Dexter Valles

I BELIEVE

How our Beliefs Determine Life

Author: Dexter John Valles
Title: I BELIEVE: How our Beliefs Determine Life
Categories: Inspiration & Personal Growth,
Success, Motivation
Inspired by: The Holy Spirit

First Edition December 2020

DEDICATION

This book is my nineth this year and is dedicated to my loving supporters

My beloved wife
Maria P Valles

Whose Belief System has been like a Lighthouse in Stormy Seas

My darling daughter
Valerie Anne Valles

Who proves why I believe in miracles!

A Special Thanks to my Supportive Friends, Followers and Fans. You know who you are.
I deeply appreciate your encouragement.
*And especially **Sanjay Hiranandani** for writing such an apt Foreword to this book!*

CONTENTS

OTHER BOOKS BY THIS AUTHOR   Page 142

FOREWORD

I was delighted when I heard that Dexter is going to be writing his 9th book during these very difficult yet thought provoking days that the world has had to deal with. I have read some of his work over the last few months and hence was eagerly looking forward to this book. It however came as a big surprise when he asked me to write a foreword for the book. I've had the good fortune of knowing Dexter for the better parts of our lives and each time we meet its always good fun and a chat that leaves you wanting more.

I've spent 30 years in Industry by and large providing services because I believe when you are in the services world you provide value from within you as against providing value from within a box when you are in the products world. It's in services that you have to believe in yourself first before you can make anyone even come close to believing in your beliefs.

Dexter the author of this book has had several years of experience bringing practical knowledge blended with his zest to be continuously learning and adding the learning to his ethos in what he does at the workplace. The highlight of what I know of Dexter is that he is at his best when he is telling what he knows.

It has not always been easy for people to see how their work affects the world but this work by Dexter at a time when the world needs to believe in itself will be an eye opener for those who believed that dreaming is possible only with your eyes shut. This book will make you believe that when you dream with your eyes open you can make them possible.

To quote a few lines from the book that caught my imagination….” Just knowing that you can choose to follow your heart right into the deepest valley of your life and chase it to the top of the mountains, is such a liberating feeling of freedom. Freedom to be the best you can ever be, way beyond the limits and boundaries of claustrophobic beliefs born and raised in the shadow of your soul and barely ignited by the flame of your spirit”

This book will make you believe in your infinite potential…. Read on and “you will believe in yourself and you will be unstoppable.”

SANJAY HIRANANDANI
Founder EFHx
An Enterprise From Home Xchange

INTRODUCTION

Have you noticed that whatever you believe in often comes true? Well our belief system is one of the most powerful guiding factors which influence, determine and define our lives. Our beliefs are things that we consider to be true and the way they play out in our lives is because in our minds we have allowed these beliefs to become the guiding principles which influence our values, our behaviour and our attitude to life. Which when we act on, more often than not we find that everything we believe in, turns out to be true. The only problem is that it's not really true. What is true is that since we believe certain things to be true or false, right or wrong, we play them out in our lives as if they were true or false, right or wrong and base our decisions on them. Thus, manifesting these beliefs into our life.

It might sound a little complex but it's really simple. For example, how many of you believe that you can become the Prime Minister or President of your country? Of course, when you were asked this question in school you probably said Yes, I want to become the Prime Minister or President! But was that a belief or just a wish? What do you think now?

Similarly, do you believe that you can be the richest person in the world or do you believe that you can be the happiest person in the world? Or do you believe that you can own the most expensive car in the world? Well, if you do, you shall and if you don't you won't!

I BELIEVE

Beliefs are the bedrock of our behaviour, drawn from how our choices and decisions are influenced by them.

In this book, we are going to take a closer look at our Belief Systems. How they impact our lives. How they transfer to others. And how to examine their validity, reframe them, channel them consciously and keep leveraging their power to deliver the dreams we believe in!

Just So You Know.......
These are the Seeds of Life you Sow.

"Your belief system is said to be the invisible force behind your behavior. Together with a host of other factors such as your attitude, personality, your genetic makeup and your habits, your belief system is one of the strongest forces that affects any decision that you are making."

"**Limiting Beliefs** break you down and make you believe the lie that you can't achieve your goal. Those beliefs are rooted in fear. **Empowering Beliefs** do the opposite. They build your confidence and encourage you to take the risk and believe in a successful outcome."

PART ONE
BUILDING
BRIDGES TO LIFE

Chapter One
OBSERVING OUR WORLD

From the day we are born we continuously observe, absorb, record and store every aspect of life around us. Much of it is done unconsciously in the beginning and as life progresses some of it is done consciously too. The unconscious or subconscious stores an enormous amount of information, recording layer over layer of data from all our five senses.

As we connect with others and become aware of their experiences, we file those away too, adding to the massive data storage in our minds.

At our conscious level of storage, we keep sifting the continuously streaming information around to levels of usefulness, in order to deal with the needs of life being dealt out to us.

And store up data we do, in great volume. It is said that if our brain was a library, we could store content of over a 100million books! Isn't that truly astonishing?!

Let's trace our observation route through life. Just the observation process builds up ginormous data mountains, without the interpretation, creation of meaning, assigning value and relevance, flagging for retrieval and use in the future, layering data of the response from the environment to such use, our own reception of such response, analysis of the primary data alongside this feedback , reframing, recasting, reallocating meaning, compartmentalization and labeling metadata clusters attached to it !

So, a new born baby, sees the world for the very first time. Limited to Mom, Dad, a sibling or two, the cradle bed, the room, well mostly the ceiling, sounds, voices, tones, light, darkness, feelings - hunger, thirst, fear, relief, satisfaction, bio functions, body parts of self, odours, what Mom feels and smells like, touch, taste and a new sensation derived from attention and care of others, relationship and connection with others however finite, a strange sound from within (baby's own voice!)

Can you imagine the impact of this onslaught of information, which each one of us had to deal with? I don't remember any of it. And I'm sure, neither do you. Yet, our brains have recorded and stored each memory byte. In our unconscious mind-space.

And from then and there, we started making some meaning of life.

As we grow, we begin to become familiar with this, because it is repeated consistently and delivers comfort. The data bank sells, finds companion data, adds bulk to each experience, and just about begins to start the beginnings of predictability. Slowly predictable comfort leads to a sense of safety and this data is gradually filed away to make room for newer unpredictable, not so comfortable, not so safe data of such experiences. Like, more people, the sounds they make and how they smell and feel, appearance of more objects, new rooms, new objects in them, the larger shocking view of a whole new world outside the window, viewed from Moms arms.

Think of all your firsts; your first steps, your first day at school, your first time on a bicycle, on skates, the first time you drove your car, your first love, your first failure, your first award, your first day at college, first day at work and expectedly, the memories become clearer and sharper. But not all that different from the experiences just beyond birth. Except for piles of data already stored and matched to all fresh inputs and a greater resilience and ease to experience, receive, store, process and use.

Chapter Two
INTERACTING WITH THE WORLD WE OBSERVE

As intelligent living beings filled with curiosity about our surroundings, we long to understand, engage interpret and put to use the data we have collected on observing the world around us. It is not possible to stay quiet in a corner and simply view the world from there.

As human beings one of the first instincts we have on observing things around us, is to engage with it, to see what it feels like, to understand more intimately how the data interplays with our lives. Therefore, very soon we start examining and engaging with great curiosity what we have been observing.

You will notice this in children and even in our adult selves, that when we are presented with something, as a child may be a toy or as an adult maybe a book or something more precious, perhaps a luxury watch, our first Instinct is to look at it with great curiosity but then very soon we reach out to touch and feel it. Even to smell it and as a child, in all probability to taste it.

This is because we decide subconsciously that it is not enough to observe and notice things but also to be able to connect with the things we are observing. This connection is an important part of our learning and development process, because our lives are not wrapped up in a cocoon of observation, but our consciousness expands with curiosity in the free space of engagement, interpretation, use and understanding the application of what we learn from this connection.

We are more timid, fearful and hesitant as children to do this, having no data of such experiences. Yet the primal instinct of safety and survival along with the compelling drive to explore and discover is woven into the strands of our DNA

As we grew, our experience of thing start to change. We rarely play in the grass, roll in the mud, climb trees or such with the same energy, contact and exuberance as we did as kids. Some of us still do, but the experience isn't the same. Because we have already layered data on that in our brain and after a certain number of similar outcomes to those experiences, we close the mental book on them. We file them away with notes on what to expect. Curiosity diminishes. We develop a framework around them. A framework we access whenever needed to deal with what we recognize as similar experiences in the future.

This is where our belief system takes over, telling us what's true of the experience, regardless of what's new. Instead, our mindspace is now occupied with collecting data of totally new experiences which are important or at least immediately accessible and engaging to our lives.

Have you noticed how little we are enamoured of things once they are "not new" like even a prized car, posh new house, travel by airplane, new laptop, new mobile phone, new gizmos, new spouse......err....pardon me....most newness fades and fails to charm us later. We sometimes even forget we have them. Because we now have enough data on them, perhaps too much. And we have spent enough time engaging with them, filing away additional data to layer atop the existing.

We believe we know enough. And sometimes are surprised to find new aspects or features of these much later. Emotional data though when attached to plain old data, make them memorable and retrievable. We call it sentiment.

There are times a sight, a smell or a note of music transport us right into our past, weaving and burrowing into piles of old data, to reach the precise location of a sentimental memory. What has all this got to do with what we believe in? Well, the short answer to that question is, sentiment retains the belief of the preciousness of that old data, now a memory. And even though filed away, is easily retrieved when that belief of the long ago past is visited unconsciously by the present.

So, it would appear that, all our observations and experiences of engagements are framed with certain values, as being valuable to us in some way, and are filed away in belief cabinets, which decide how true they are to represent our lives.

I BELIEVE

If you were asked today to describe what experiences of the past have served to define your life, your brain would be pulling open those cabinets and retrieving what it believes served best to secure your life to the meaning you now describe with value. These might not necessarily be true, but they are your truths. And if you minutely track their footprints across your life, you will find that many of your decisions and actions carried these truths on their shoulders.

For me, it meant who I wished to befriend, who I considered wise or not, who could be relied on and who was unreliable, what mattered to success, what distracted from it, who deserved my respect and who didn't, who was worthy of teaching me and who was not, the importance of local language mastery other than English, films, songs, cuisines, dress sense, demeanor, attitude.

Ah, there is a critical word. **Attitude**. The gateway of beliefs into the courtyard of life.

Viktor Frankl wrote about Attitude, among several other life truths and experiences, in one of the worst ever places to learn these. The Nazi concentration camps. A survivor of the Holocaust and the notorious Auschwitz concentration camp, Viktor Frankl's book "Man's Search for Meaning" is a classic tribute to Hope from the Holocaust.

He goes on to say that despite the inhuman circumstances there was always room to make decisions based on your self determination of the choices you had and how you wished to approach them with your attitude, which was the ultimate freedom of a human being. To be able to make that choice.

Chapter Three
OPINIONS, JUDGEMENTS, BELIEFS, INTERPRETATIONS

This is where things get interesting. This is where you are saying to yourself. Aha! now we are getting somewhere and just because you read the title of this chapter.

This is because, as you have just read and already concluded, that we cannot just observe and engage with life without forming an opinion and sitting in judgement of the product of our interpretation, as presented to what we believe to be true. We just cannot help doing this, because it helps us make decisions and take actions based on it. Without completing this circuit, we would feel hijacked by the vast overwhelming volume of data and paralyzed into inaction.

By the process of interpreting the experience along with our value and belief systems, we form our opinion about it, which quickly becomes a temporary judgement which is treated as final until we are presented with starkly different experiences and outcomes which contradict or substantially jolt our earlier judgements off their rails.

Once we are satisfied with the closure of this loop, we seek and find substantive but not exhaustively complete proof of our judgements and so pronounce them to be true. Our Belief System then adds this to its vast repository. To be called on whenever required.

Let's make this easy to understand.
Try and recall the first time you tried to ride a bicycle. Or skate. Or swim. Or drive a car. Or play a musical instrument. Initially you would have observed the experience keenly, as a bystander. And it would have looked so simple. Then you tried it yourself convinced this was easy to do. Right? Wrong. And you are smiling now. Because, when you tried it yourself, it was so darned hard, difficult, complicated and perfectly nasty.

This strange experience follows these famous four steps of learning:

Step 1: Unconscious Incompetence: You don't know that you can't do it right.

Step 2: Conscious Incompetence: You now know that you can't do it right

Step 3: Conscious Competence: You learn to do it right

Step 4: Unconscious Competence: You practice it so much, that you can do it right in your sleep. Or so it seems! Guess what happened between Step 1 and Step 4? You're right. You altered your opinion, judgements and belief about your capability and competence.

I BELIEVE

Step 1 led to a collapse and crash of your belief. Step 2 (if you persisted) led to a temporary reforming of your belief, with a rider, that it was something you needed to work on, not drop as un-doable.

Step 3 helped to alter the entire belief in a more reasoned way with structured steps to validate the belief in stages, rather than jump to the end belief.

Step 4 created a new assured belief similar to Pre-Step 1, but now backed by validated experiences.

So a decision to say ride a bike based on a Pre-Step 1 belief and a Post-Step 4 belief would have remarkably different outcomes, despite the end belief being outwardly more or less the same!

What do you think happened?
Well, you tested your belief safely when you enrolled to learn, rather than execute with bravado. By testing your beliefs, you were confronted by some difficult truths. Truths which knocked your earlier judgement and beliefs off the rails. And helped reframe them to being useful in any decisions and actions you may hence choose based on that belief. The question is: What if you had not tested your belief safely first?

The question following that question is "**Are you acting on your life on any such untested beliefs?**"

What if the consequences of such actions are not yet visible or known to you?

This brings us to a fundamental part of our belief system. **Faith.**

When our belief in something that rings so strong and true, that we waive the need for challenging its authenticity, integrity, accuracy and even its existence, well, that belief becomes Faith. Or even Blind Faith. Like the existence of a powerful and alive Universe, a mysterious governing superpower called God.

There are other fundamental beliefs founded by distinctions and separation of society by virtue of religion, race, colour and country. Faith however is a founding fundamental belief.

As we grow in Faith, we grow in Trust of that Faith, often without our own conclusive evidence of it. We are happy to accept the testimony of others as evidence of that Faith. And our data base is layered with all kinds of invisible evidence interpreted and judged into confirmation of that Faith.

In fact, if we are challenged by an opposing point of view or worse, by a person holding an opposing point of view, we feel personally assaulted, and more often than not, launch into battle, without the armour of evidence, but armed to the teeth with our belief.

I call this a fundamental belief because, and you will quickly agree, this belief utterly alters the very fundamentals of how we view, engage, interpret, measure and judge the world. Always believing we are the True Centre of Universal Truth, and everyone else is dealt with based on their distance from or proximity to the truth. Our truth. Our own other beliefs are generously coloured by this fundamental belief. Our Core Beliefs constantly inhale these fumes like life giving oxygen.

Let's take an example.

You grow up battling inequities and establish a balanced, reasoned, fair and just way of life. You are the founder of sterling life principles, which you preach widely and practice too. You rise in esteem and are soon a role model.
Your core beliefs seem to have worked well for you. Then one day your only child, announces she has found a life partner. She describes him. A truly wonderful person. You are excited, happy and grateful.

And then, ask the all-important question. Guess what that question is?

The answer to that question needs to fit perfectly into your fundamental belief.

Otherwise, nothing else matters. No amount of evidence can surmount the mountains of no-evidence blind belief, if the fundamental belief is crossed.

Unless of course every other Core Belief you live by, rises to strike down the unreasonable blind belief. Which is an incredibly devastating blow, often ending in ripping apart life from almost every seam.

Have you known families experiencing this? Terrible outcomes emerge to drag life over the coals forever. What are these outcomes? Let's see

Outcome 1: Permission may not be granted and life settles into sullen, wounded silence, damaged beyond repair. Redressal measures to meet approved fundamental beliefs, end up disastrously, shredding all good intentions to pieces.

Outcome 2: Permission may be granted with accompanying malice, by breaking the relationship permanently. Much grief and sorrow follows. Guilt, shame engulfs both sides. Disgrace to the family which was quoted as being staved off, now actually turns true.

Outcome 3: This is a really tough one. Life is sacrificed rather than compromise on the fundamental blind belief.

And everything that was believed to be good and true, turns out to be really bad and fake.

Unless you were wise enough to have added another fundamental belief to your blind belief.

I BELIEVE

"You are not supposed to save people from their lives. Everyone has a fundamental right to their own life"

You may guide, advise, debate, demonstrate, counsel, negotiate, bargain. Then learn to listen with empathy. Find the vulnerable human being in yourself and the other. And release your blind rigidity of belief to the greater power of the Universe.

Easier said than done.

In her book *Daring Greatly – How the Courage to be Vulnerable Transforms the Way We Live, Love, Parent and Lead, the author Brene Brown* writes about the Vulnerability Armory. She writes that while growing up as children we protected ourselves from being hurt and made to feel small. According to her, we hid behind our Thoughts, Emotions, Behaviours using them as shields. But now as adults we need to step out from behind those shields and face the world with courage, to claim who we really are and want to be. She says "We must take off the armour, put down the weapons, show up, and let ourselves be seen."

PART TWO

CORE BASES OF BELIEFS

Chapter Four
Belief Base #1
BELIEF ABOUT THE WORLD

Our World views are what decides how we deal with it, including some quirky ones like: What makes the World Turn, Is the World Round, Are We Alone, Does the Universe Matter, How significant are we, Do we really Matter?!

This is a Fundamental Belief Base. It grounds our very fundamental beliefs about the very world we live in. All other beliefs either grow from these or are influenced by them.

By the time we experience how life tests and challenges us, we develop theories and beliefs about life itself and the world which offers this life to us. From these or with these, we develop most of our actionable beliefs which determine how we live the why of life.

Let's take a closer look at the range of these beliefs. They live on both sides of the fence in fields of limiting and empowering beliefs, and some precariously on the fence.

Our World (and by association, Life itself) is:
- ➢ Unforgiving
- ➢ About Survival of the Fittest
- ➢ Sometimes good, more often bad
- ➢ Magical only if you believe in it.
- ➢ A Ruthlessly brutal battlefield
- ➢ A Miraculous place
- ➢ Chaotic, Random, Unpredictable
- ➢ Governed by Luck, either Good or Bad
- ➢ Subject to destiny or fate, regardless of effort

This is just an illustrative short list. It does paint the picture though!

How do these beliefs infiltrate, embed themselves, influence and direct our behaviour and actions ultimately determining our life?

Let's take a few examples from (the very short list of indicative beliefs) above and see some of the possible ways they could and often do play out.

See if you recognize yourself or some people you know from the brief notes about these beliefs

Unforgiving
May make you unforgiving too, to match what the world is. You may demand perfection or delay action beyond usefulness, for fear of retribution.

Applied across life, may make you rigid, inflexible, a fault finder, driving yourself into isolation and leading people with a whip.

Empathy, forgiveness, reconciliation, compromise, working with shortcomings are possibly the most difficult to practice

Survival of the Fittest
Life is a race to prove that only the fittest survive. Your competitiveness may lead you to destroy the "opposition"
You could become obsessed with acquiring power in order to be the fittest, fastest, strongest.

People you consider unfit don't get your attention unless they agree to be whipped into shape by you.

People who are supremely fit in whatever they do, become competitive targets to be vanquished, rather than become allies.

Collaboration will only be at your terms. Cooperation is the last resort. Standing tall and victorious is as vital as life itself.

Sometimes good, more often bad

You would probably be living life looking over your shoulder for signs of the "bad" catching up.

You rarely are grateful for the good in life, because you expect the bad

You are relieved when things go wrong!

You don't prepare well enough for permanence or the longevity of good things

You become a cynic and are skeptical of all "good stories"

Magical only if you believe in it.

Let the magic begin! What a wonderful world we see when we believe it is magical.

You are likely to be a super optimist. Always believing that magic makes everything right. And yes indeed, it does. Though it probably isn't the magic in the world, but the magic within you, which is conjuring miracles every day.

Optimism is a great emotion to ride on. It allows you to believe in the best, of every circumstance and in everyone. You could be the one to whom people turn to when life gets the better of them. You may also sail through troubles like they don't exist. Check if you sometimes act and do things which don't truly connect with or accept the darkness of reality. It may make you irrelevant. The magic of the world must live and deal with the darkness. Like light needs night.

Living on the fumes of magic could push you to live in a bubble in which others find no place. On the other hand, believing in the magic within you, can transport you to bring that belief to colour a dreary life, when the very ordinariness and routines of life bring grey and gloomy skies to visit your day.

A Ruthlessly Brutal Battlefield

So, life is a battle. Bloody, fierce, live or die, kill or be killed. To the victor, the spoils.

As an old saying goes: In the jungle, when the sun rises, whether you are a lion or a gazelle, hit the ground running!

Blowing the bugle of war each morning can bring out the winning warrior in you. You charge into the day. Work through each challenge fiercely. Cut them down to size. Brandish the blueprint, marshal the troops, load your weapons and fire! What's a battlefield without the roar of canons or the shriek of missiles.

By the end of the day, you walk through the bodies of the vanquished and the valorous. Then you plant your flag of victory, right through the heart of the enemy. And the market applauds. Just as they do when another flag on another day is driven through yours!!

Chaotic, Random, Unpredictable

Since this is true for you, you probably don't need to plan or make alternative plans. Plan A is just in case the world in its randomness lets it through. Not that it will happen again. So like a highly strung and nervous goal keeper at the post, watching a furious game from a distance, you are always prepared for the field of dreams to rotate to you and stretch for the ball flying past your head.

On the other hand if you enjoy "going with the flow" no matter where and how it goes, you probably thrive on chaos, randomness and the sheer unpredictability of life as you see it to be. And more often than not, make it to be. Providing delightful proof of your pudding!

The way you lead could mirror this belief. While the mix of chaos, randomness and unpredictability can throw up genius strategy and fabulously unexpected results, you may want to examine the other truths like burnout, disarray, distress, delusion and even disconnect that come as part of the package.

The smart way to navigate with success would be to find the calm with the chaos, the pattern within randomness and the harness to ride unpredictability!

Subject to luck, destiny or fate, regardless of effort

You keep looking for "signs", "omens" rather than secure your decisions and actions for successful delivery

I BELIEVE

You don't examine what went wrong when things fail You don't put in the extra effort, since you feel it doesn't count anyway

If you've experienced "good luck" you expect to live a charmed life.

You consider people struggling in life as "bad luck" and stay far from them

You blame failure on the stars

You adopt strange practices and rituals to appeal to and appease the "Gods" of luck, fate and destiny.

These beliefs become our mental structures, our frames of mind and our mindsets as we practice these beliefs. Our decisions and actions are framed and coloured by these beliefs.

Have you experienced this in your life?

Perhaps if you were to pay attention to the additional information accompanying the consequences of these actions and process them separately (not easy at all when beliefs become hardwired habits) you would find a way to more options and altered beliefs.

Chapter Five
Belief Base # 2
BELIEF ABOUT LIFE & LIVING

Do you investigate the circumstance of every passing moment? To gather data, organize it, arrange it into meaningful clusters, form connections, interpret, add meaning and set decision parameters and guidelines?

I don't! And surely you do not too. If we did, it would be excruciatingly difficult to get past the day. We probably did so when we began life, even before we were fully conscious of it. We observed flow, patterns, actions, results and developed some kind of inner commentary on it. Then we filed it away for retrieval when required to refer to it during other moments. We have talked about this right at the start of this book too. Right?

All this processed data, both conscious and unconscious, gradually at first and then quickly formed into reasoned assumptions, or ways in which we figured out various bits of life. These processed bits of life we observed, repeated, in various degrees of similarity. We also figured out along the way, how to bend the assumptions we made to suit the degrees of similarity or even dissimilarity. Am I doing okay this far?

Well, guess what we did about all this figuring out? We put them into neat little mental boxes of uniquely processed data. Then learned to add further processed and refined data across time into these boxes. And voila! We made each box reasonably watertight and called them our beliefs. Or at least, what we though, to be true to our lives and how we were living it.

Yes, that made life a whole lot easier. Beliefs gathered values around them. Values are what we considered valuable to supporting our beliefs. To keep what's true, true and what's false, false. And between these we operated life, for every belief. Making decisions through these templates of thoughts and the emotions we built around them.

So now, we were able to sense and feel our beliefs and values even before we were aware of them in our thoughts. What a great bonus this was, and still is! We now can almost automatically act on our beliefs and values, delivering results we approve of, leaving room for higher order examination and processing life, to stretch, grow, develop and skill ourselves beyond the foundations we lay.

And this repeats. Layer over layer. As we climb the mountain of life, atop which lies the pinnacle of success.

The great discovery we make along the way up, is that our belief footsteps find foothold in the belief footsteps of others who have climbed and claimed the mountain too. We add our footprints to those, to leave them for others who shall follow us up that mountain. Our teams, our children, our flock of believers.

And so life goes on. Smoothly, securely and with growing confidence. We soon become experts in delivering our beliefs into results. Until they don't. Until they deliver strangely. Until someone points out the flaws in our results. Until we slip way down the mountain, just when we are within inches of the summit!

Whipping out our Book of Beliefs, we find to our utter surprise that we've actually followed them all! So, what went wrong? Maybe we should be checking our assumptions. The assumptions which were clarified into our beliefs. If those assumptions were flawed, then our beliefs as true as they may be, won't work out as we require them too. So, while everything seems right, the results are wrong. Our values soaked in emotions attached to our beliefs, refuse permission to shift or change.

So, we try again, harder. And fall harder. Unless our emotions shift to allow us to reexamine our assumptions, our beliefs just won't deliver.

How then do we shift our emotions? Well, by listening to what they are saying. And how they colour the way we paint our beliefs into our actions.

I BELIEVE

Read more about emotions, emotional signatures, emotional intelligence to identify your emotions in play. Some of these are in an annexure at the end of this book.

Our emotions swirl around protecting, preserving and growing our life, and the beliefs which we have installed into the framework of our decision making and action plans.

Reexamining our assumptions which form our key beliefs can often feel like threatening their validity and very existence. Not a lot of happy emotion there!

Have you been in such a position? Of-course you have. And so, have I. What do you remember of any particularly significant moments which brought in clear and stark confrontations of your beliefs?

What did you feel?
What did you do?
What was your process of course correction?
What did you learn?
How did the lessons of that or those experiences actually carry across your journey?
What have you done recently to review your assumptions and beliefs?

Let's take a closer look at our assumptions across these.

Assumptions start tentatively as hypotheses and then over a pretty short period of time and experience, based on how much is the volume and pace of life for you, are held to be true or false. Consciously or unconsciously. These become our Beliefs:

Reflect and write about your own Assumptions about these areas of Life
Success-Failure,
Equality- Inequality (Rich-Poor,
Privileged-Underprivileged) ,
Rules, Regulations, Reward, Punishment
Intelligence Determinants-Rational Mind, Emotional Brain

A few from my own vast global library of experiences, both past, archived and current are :

Success-Failure
You either succeed or fail. There is no halfway
Success leads to fame, prosperity, happiness
Failure leads to struggles, sacrifices, poverty and unhappiness
You need to fail in order to succeed
If you have never failed before it's due to happen.
Winners are successful, failure is for losers.
Hard work is essential to success. Lack of it leads to failure.
Success is necessary to feel good about yourself. Failure

leads to feelings of shame and guilt.

Fear is a key emotion driving success or failure.

Fear leads to failure

Conquer fear in order to succeed.

Success enriches life. Failure depletes it.

Culture, Race, Religion, Upbringing, Gender determines the rate of success or failure

Learn Success from the success and failure of others

Equality- Inequality (Rich-Poor, Privileged Underprivileged)

This is a natural state of the world.

Everyone cannot be equal in every way

Accept the imbalance and use it to work on your own goals

It is important that the world is unequal.

Jobs across the stratas of life, can only be done in an unequal world.

Culture, Race, Religion, Upbringing lead to inequalities, privileges, provision and deprivation of status and standard of living.

Genders are unequal.

Genders are equal but not in the same way.

Gender inequality complement each other's strengths and challenges

Social order demands gender inequality

Genders must be treated as equal even though they are unequal.

Inequality impacts success and defines failure

Inequality is not a permanent state of life

Inequality is a great motivator or conversely, a demotivator

Rules, Regulations, Reward, Punishment

Rules and Regulations are essential to life

Life must be lived within boundaries

Boundaries help control life

People must live their lives and roles within boundaries

Progress is based on following rules.

Rules and Regulations moderate, control, harness and direct effort.

Rules and Regulations encumber life and performance

Rules and Regulations restrict creativity and imagination

Rules and Regulations are meant only for the undisciplined

Rules and Regulations are the cause of fear and uncertainty.

Boundaries create narrow viewpoints and ways of living

Boundaries restrict abundance

Rules and Regulations need to be more about the spirit rather than the law.

Unwritten Rules are the most important ones

Every Rule needs to be in black and white

People breaching or breaking rules need to be punished to ensure order, control and discipline.

People maintaining rules and regulations must be acknowledged but not rewarded.

People protecting rules and regulations from being breached need to be recognized and may be rewarded depending on merit.

Punishment is a necessary tool of good governance.

Intelligence Determinants-Rational Mind, Emotional Brain

We are schooled to believe that being rational is better than being emotional. Somehow that grave belief has resulted in much trauma. In 1995 Daniel Goleman was the first to write about Emotional Intelligence and the advantages of being emotionally intelligent over being just intelligent. This led to several conversations, research and the study of the mind, including the opening up of studies in neuroscience to understand the mysteries of the mind and especially how emotional chemicals influence our feelings, thoughts and actions. Emotional Intelligence or its measure EQ, is shown in several studies, to matter as much and more than the measure of one's IQ. You can read more about this and how it is practiced in life, by simply browsing the internet. Look in the annexure to this book for useful links to Emotional Intelligence sites.

Yet our belief systems still hold Assumptions we grew up with on the matter of being Rational or Emotional (now understood as being emotionally intelligent) Some of these are:

A Rational Mind delivers best results.
A Rational Mind is free of bias and prejudice.

A Rational Mind needs to be cultivated. Often by suppressing the Emotional Mind.

Emotions are a sign of weakness.

Women are more emotional. Men are more rational. Strength and Power are supported, nurtured and grown by a Rational Mind.

Intelligence is the product of a trained rational mind

Emotions cloud rational reasoning.

These are all some examples of the assumptions forming our beliefs. You can certainly add to them from your own life experiences.

It's not important though, to merely write these, but also important and valuable to identify the Beliefs, Values, Emotions and Actions arising through these.

As we go through this book, you will come across some guided opportunities to do just this!

Chapter Six
Belief Base #3
BELIEF ABOUT SELF

Belief about My Life (Who Am I, Who Can I Be, My Worthiness)
Belief about My Role in Life (What I Am Supposed to be Doing)
Belief about Other People (And how they Relate to Me)

Our belief system would be handicapped severely if we have not formed beliefs about ourselves.

After all, we are the Center of our Universe and everything gets measured from there. Isn't that so? It's been true for me for almost forever. Until I discovered that the Universe was filled with other Centers. We are so integral to our story, that we can't be just one of the characters in it. We are the main protagonist. The central character. The lead actor. Add to that, the writer, the publisher, the producer, the director and the casting coordinator.

The Book of My Life would probably not have space for anyone else. As funny and odd as that seems, in a strange way, it's quite true. We are, by default, obsessed with

ourselves. A large portion of what we do, even when we do it for others, is because it is about us. The returns of all our efforts and engagements must run back to us. It takes a lot of conscious unwiring and rewiring of our life's agenda, to let go of our ego, to expand our presence and influence yet shrink our returns on such investment. As we turn that corner, our belief about self, reforms and then transforms our lives.

Let's take a look at ourselves and what we believe to be true to our life as we live it.

You could break it down to the A, B, C described by me, as you read further. You could also make your own personal list. In fact, I encourage you to do that too.

Here are my A, B and C and I shall elaborate on each as we go along this path.

    A. Belief about My Life (Who Am I, Who Can I Be, My Worthiness)
    B. Belief about My Role in Life (What I Am Supposed to be Doing)
    C. Belief about Other People (And how they Relate to Me)

Sounds familiar?

Rings a whole lot of bells I'm sure!

I BELIEVE

Here goes:

A) Belief about My Life (Who Am I, Who Can I Be, My Worthiness)

We are always the best version of ourselves, in our own mind. And then we connect with a bump in life. The first of several to come. Speed breakers, potholes, diversions, roadblocks, steep inclines, we can go on.

After that first encounter, it feels like a blow to the solar plexus of our confidence and the flurry of blows that follow knock the breath and belief out of us

We jump from one end of the spectrum to the other. What was good about us, is now bad. What worked well, won't work anymore. Who I am, Who I can be and My Worthiness take a terrible beating. In our own minds, more than in truth. The sheer disappointment and frustration with how our expectations from ourselves have crashed, pummel our ego with punishing blows.

It now becomes the new reality.

Our primal caveman instincts are roused as danger to our projected success threatens the way forward. Survival replaces success strategies, doubt and suspicion replace confidence and trust, hesitance replaces flow, caution freezes courage, fear becomes a companion.

It's strange yet true, that as humans, we dwell more on what is wrong than what is right with ourselves and our lives. Part of the evolution of our species. Growing up too, you would have found, that all progress has been tied securely to "improvement" of what wasn't strong enough or good enough, not about further strengthening what is right and strong about us. Our education and assessment of performance at work too, makes this a greater descriptor of who we are than anything else. We are now known by what we cannot do. And soon, we become what we cannot do.

It takes a lot of Conscious Coaching to shake this off, before such beliefs grow deep roots into our minds and hearts. Once convinced in "what we know and feel about ourselves" becomes our inner truth. This is very hard to change. But it does, eventually, with some work on presenting, practicing and persisting with the opposing beliefs.

Some beliefs and counter beliefs (also beliefs, but in the opposite direction) could look like this.

I am perfect in everything I do
I am flawed.
I always make mistakes
I cannot get anything right

I BELIEVE

I am strong, powerful and a winner
I am weak and powerless
I can never win
I am a loser

I am special and people seek me.
I am ordinary
I have nothing special
I am not special
I have nobody who values me.
I am useless

I am valued and my opinion matters
My voice makes a difference
I have no real value and my opinion doesn't count
I do not have a voice and it doesn't make any difference
even if I did.

I am in control of my life and my destiny.
I determine what happens in my life
I cannot control things in my life.
Things happen to me. I cannot change them

I am talented, skilled, capable, knowledgeable and worthy of
great success
I am nothing
I cannot make things work
I don't have the right talents, skills, knowledge

I am incapable
I am unworthy of success

I am destined for fame and success.
I can never be famous
Even if I was famous, I would lose it.
I can never be successful.
I am a failure already.

I am going to be a force to reckon with.
I can never be a force to reckon with
I am not worthy of being someone.
I am destined to be a nobody

Are you identifying with these yet? Pick the ones you feel most describe your beliefs or "inner truths" and trace their journeys from where they probably began. Ask questions about the options you could have given yourself. Don't try to undo the past, but note down those options for the road ahead. Keep them handy.

It takes time to flip a belief. So be gentle with yourself. But be of firm resolve too. Just remember that the future is not yet decided, until it becomes your present, and you are fully present in it ! You always have first rights to your own life.

That's a law of the universe.

B) Belief about My Role in Life (What I Am Supposed to be Doing)

My belief about who I am, who I can be and whether or not I am worthy, seeps into what I believe my role is in life.

Could be anything But it forms the Vision we have of ourselves in our minds. We play that out unless that vision is replaced by another. It depends on how much we subscribe to it. How much we believe in it. To be true. To be our truth.

What have you believed in? How is life delivering on those beliefs? **Could any or several of these roles describe your life?** They are NOT opposites of each other, though some may seem so. This list is very short, so do add to it.

A Leader	A Follower
A Somebody	A Nobody
A Creator	A Consumer
A Teacher	A Student
A Healer	A Destroyer
A Provider	A Disruptor
An Employer	An Employee
An Entrepreneur	A Worker
A Guide	A Coach
A Resource	A Researcher

Add names of other roles you know of, to those listed. Leave out biological roles. They come naturally. Though within those, you may find the ones listed above featuring through them.

One way to reach a good understanding on the roles you play, would be to ask others how they see you, and note those descriptors down.

See if you can connect them all together to allow roles to emerge from within them. This is the story of your life. The one you have been writing, knowingly or unknowingly.

Don't forget to add your own perceptions of your life to these. Some of your own perceptions may be in subtle to sharp contrast with those received as feedback. What will you do? I suggest you mark your perceptions into "aspirational" roles. You get to not only see how differently people view you, but also how far your beliefs have travelled into your life!

TEN POINTS TO REFLECT ON

1. You may have multiple Roles. Which are they?
2. Describe each Role you see yourself in. You may certainly add to the list given here.
3. Explain WHY you see yourself in each Role you feature in, regardless how big or small these Roles appear in your life.
4. What are the actions you usually demonstrate in these Roles ?

5. Which Roles do you see emerge as your Top 3 to 5 Roles across your life?

6. How are they impacting your life? See if you can list the impact for each individual Role.

7. Which single Role underpins almost all of your behaviour, decisions and actions? This is your Go-To Role. What does it say to you?

8. What does it say ABOUT you? What do you want to do about it?

9. Which Role or Roles would you prefer to embody and demonstrate?

10. If you were a child, what advice would you give this child? Would YOU act on this advice too? What will it cost you to do that?

Keep these Reflections in mind (hopefully you would have written them down in a journal) when doing the exercise on The Magnificent Seven Questions in Chapter Eight, which is about Acting On Beliefs-Choices, Decisions, Actions

C) Belief about Other People (And how they Relate to Me)

Our belief system would not be complete without what we believe about others and how these others connect, engage with and impact us.

This allows us to pre decide how to deal with them in our relationships. Which by the way, we label as formal, informal, personal, professional, casual, long term, transient to name some of them. Even before we probably understand the relationship fully, our beliefs about them, decide how we behave in them and the decisions we make when in them.

The people we allocate into these types of belief boxes, find themselves living in them for as long a time as our beliefs find support from the outcomes of our categorized patterns of behaviour. Until of course we are dramatically aroused to change the box, we continue with what seems to work. Even if closer examination would uncover that much better results could be delivered if we altered our beliefs about the relationship. Mediocrity seems to suffice in certain areas of life. Which is a belief in itself.

So, you may decide not to generously tip a restaurant service, on a casual drive by on an unfamiliar route which you are not likely to use again. This relationship does not count you think. Even if the server is left unhappy. They should expect this to happen on the highway, you console yourself. Unless of course, you discover you didn't retrieve your credit card after making the payment, or worse, left your wallet itself under the napkin.

You would have heard people say, they are taken for granted. May you think you are. Maybe you take people for granted. This is because your assumptions about how the relationship should be delivered, received and accepted have formed into your belief. Once you practice it enough without receiving any pushback, well, you just keep doing it . Your belief settles comfortably into its actions. And lives there unconsciously thereafter.

So, we believe, our family must stand by us, understand our circumstances, manage our moods, compensate for us, step up and support us, be available, pay attention, roll with our punches and love us to the moon and back. Why? Because that's what families do. So, no need to check how the relationship is doing.

Yet, this is not the same with the Boss or the Client. There the belief system has incredible contrasts. Quite the opposite you may say. And at the receiving end of some really brutal behaviour, you too don't dare have a conversation about how you wish to be treated. Why? There's another belief system driven by our belief about hierarchy and how power structures work. Belief Base #2 comes to life.

Every now and then, you should make an effort to examine your relationships and check their vital signs for health, happiness and growth

You may wind up challenging your beliefs, which would be a good thing. No point owing a great fierce dog to guard the house, if it decides to sleep soundly on the weekend. The same way with our belief system. The more it sleeps undisturbed, well, the less effectively it works, in a constantly churning world.

Chapter Seven
Belief Base # 4
BELIEF ABOUT THE FUTURE

Tough as it is to navigate the present, it's amazing how we obsess with what is in store for us in the future. We have notions about it too. Notions we have nurtured across the past and present. Notions about the future we have cultured to becoming Beliefs, to be true, regardless of how it actually plays out.

We believe we can create the future or force it to "behave" with a steady predictability delivering a carefully constructed life. This despite acknowledging the unpredictability and fluid state of flow of our best laid plans. All of this courtesy a Belief Blueprint we have designed or rather etched with nearly indelible ink to meet the constructs of a future we want to have, possess and inhabit.

What do you believe about the Future?

Let's do something interesting Write 10 words (even 3-word phrases count as 1 word !!) that come to mind when you think about the future. We shall assume the future to mean beyond the next 5 years and up to 4 decades ahead.

I BELIEVE

Why 4 decades? Well, it's a random number, but in a way it represents around half a lifetime. Enough to witness significant progress and change. And for some of us, just at the edge or just beyond our own lifespan.

Once you've done that, look at them for a few minutes and see if you can connect and shape them into some sort of statement of belief.

It is useful to understand here, that what we are referring to as Beliefs about the Future are actually Assumptions we make about the future. Since we have no way of verifying them to be true or false. They are hypotheses we pose, hoping to prove them to be true.

From these assumptions we extract our beliefs. Our Beliefs are what we believe to be true despite the lack of evidence. These beliefs or truths of life give us a sense of tangible purpose to guide and direct life. And predict the Future.

Back to my 10 words. *(an illustrative example)*

My 10 words about the Future could be these (*you can see I am not counting words here !) :*

Challenging, Ecologically altered, Artificially Intelligent Tech, Medically advanced Genetic Coding & Engineering, Advanced Space Outreach, Globally merged markets, Unified Political Geographies, Ideologically Defined Human Colonies,

Bio-Synthetic Food and Nutrition, Discovery and Mining of Alien Elements, Minerals and Metals.

So, for me, this could be stitched together to form a picture of the Future as follows:

Stated as beliefs, these are assumptions which although unproven, serve to be close to the truth we imagine.

Here goes.

"I Believe the Future is going time be challenging to human life, in an ecologically altered planet. A New Earth with unprecedented paradigms of transformation in technology with Artificial Intelligence being the core driver of everyday life.

I Believe that the Human Being itself will bear the testimony of advanced Genetic Engineering to advance lifespan; Bio-Synthetic food and nutrition to improve health, develop resistance and immunity to dreaded diseases, add super strength to body and spark new neural circuits of an highly advanced and intelligent mind.

I Believe Man will traverse Space, discovering the secrets of the Universe through advanced Space Outreach programs, mining alien planets for their minerals and metals, establishing living colonies on planets so far unknown to us.

I BELIEVE

I Believe this world will be truly transformed with Unified Political Geographies, ideologically clustered communities defined by their ideologies rather than race or colour or living location.

I Believe this world will need great strength of body and mind to live in. Only the super skilled shall survive and thrive. Superman shall be the new Man. Star Trek shall be actual chronicles of our times."

So looking at the assumptions I have postulated about the future, I would list my actual illustrative Belief Statement about the Future as follows:

"I Believe the Future shall be extraordinarily fierce and challenging, complex and complicated as a consequence of a highly advanced and evolved life - scientifically, technologically, biologically, socially, geo-politically, where only the competent and competitive shall survive and thrive in a world of constant furious change."

What's your Belief Statement looking like?

What are your actions likely to be to influence and drive the World today to embrace the World of tomorrow? The one you believe it is going to be.

PART THREE

BRINGING

BELIEFS TO LIFE

Chapter Eight
ACTING ON BELIEFS- CHOICES, DECISIONS, ACTIONS

We have seen how valuable it is to reflect on our Assumptions, Beliefs, Values and Emotions and they way they are influencers of our behaviour and life itself.

Let us undertake and exercise which will help ground these reflections into a useful document of purpose and application.

Step 1: In your diary, list each individual one of your assumptions turned beliefs, as a statement, inside a circle.

Step 2: Draw a larger diameter circle around this circle, and in this circle, write values attached to this belief.

Step 3: Then in an even larger concentric circle write actions arising from your beliefs and values.

Step 4: Draw several arrows pointing outwards from this circle to cloud shaped bubbles within which you need to write down all possible consequences, both real and probable, arising

from these actions. Qualify as desirable or undesirable.

Step 5: Surround this drawing by all the possible emotions you are likely to experience and are experiencing right now in this process, across your beliefs and values, and what you feel about them as well as what you feel when you engage them in life through your decisions and actions. You are doing this on each page for each key Assumption turned Belief.

Step 6: When you finish all, look across all values and emotions and list separately the common values and emotions you see across these pages. Even twice counts.

Step 7: Make a list of all the common consequences as well.

Step 8: Answer these 7 Questions (My Magnificent Seven) on the blank page alongside each set of circles. For every Belief you listed. You can summarize at the end.

The 7 Questions you may want to ask yourself are:

1) How are each of these influencing me in 5 crucial areas of my life? - My Life Goals, My Career Goals, My Image & Personal Brand Equity, My Health, My Relationships.

2) What do I need to change in my life in these areas?

3) How are my Beliefs likely to Empower, Limit or Block me?

4) What needs to shift?

5) What do I need to do to manage that shift? A) Myself B) Though the Help and Support of Others

I BELIEVE

6) What do I need to do to monitor, manage and mentor this shift?

7) How will I know if the shift itself is valid to the needs of my life?

You better keep a full book of 200 blank A4 sized pages to do this exercise. My guess is that you will need the entire book.

Understanding that your "Belief System" is throwing up challenges delivering differently than desired in your life, write down a rough Action Plan or Action Steps to reshape and reframe these Beliefs so that they work for you more than they are doing right now.

A good way to approach implementing an action plan arising from this would be by harnessing the power of Emotional Intelligence in an everyday way across your life.

EI or EQ as it is often referred to, provides the key set of competencies required to deliver real value in our lives, through how we manage our relationships and get to the results we desire.

Despite our conscious and unconscious Beliefs, Values and accompanying Emotions which tether them to our lives and behaviour, EQ can help rewire, reroute and reframe our behaviour such that our Beliefs start reframing themselves through the new lens to life provided by our experiences

The reason backing this, is that our emotions when intelligent help us to:

- ➤ Recognize who we are: what we like, don't like and what we need
- ➤ Communicate *mindfully*, clearly and effectively
- ➤ Make decisions based on the things that are most important to us
- ➤ Get motivated and take action to meet goals
- ➤ Understand and *empathize* with others
- ➤ Build Relationships that are strong, healthy and rewarding

The emotions you feel are a great indicator of your beliefs. Though there is a route by which you can figure it out. A bread crumb route of emotions, values, choices, decisions and assumptions. Leading to the House of Beliefs, built by you.

Emotions and values travel together. Your emotions and how you feel about a choice or decision or action prompted by them, tell you whether your values are being celebrated or betrayed.

Either way, these lead you to which beliefs or assumptions first put these choices into play. Once you are there, you get a chance to peep behind the belief curtains of your mind and examine the canvass being painted with the colors, biases, prejudices, judgements, rules of your belief system.

That giant canvass is the great big background of your very own theatrical stage of life. A continuously in motion

I BELIEVE

Broadway Show!! Scripted, Directed, Produced and Starring, YOU!

Here are **FIVE** ways to work through your protesting emotions and hijacked values, in order to deliver life beyond these boundaries of your Beliefs

REFRAMING YOUR BELIEF BLUEPRINT

Living Your Beliefs through a Re-Purposed Life

1: SELF

FUNDAMENTAL BELIEF: I am Worthy. Others are too.

DEVELOPMENTAL ACTIONS

1) Develop Significant Purpose in Life to have a more meaningful life. Set Life Goals.
2) Develop Courage to face Adversity with more Optimism, Ownership and Endurance. Know what it takes to see things through the rough times.
3) Develop Compassion for others and the ability to Forgive yourself and others.
4) Develop a Change Plan to Personally Make a Difference and become an Agent of Change. Take responsibility for Change.

2: OTHERS

FUNDAMENTAL BELIEF: I Support the Success of Others

DEVELOPMENTAL ACTIONS

1) Build a Spirit of Collaboration and Support. Not just co-operation. Collaboration is full engagement.
2) Be Trustworthy in everything. Especially little things. All the time.
3) Communicate with Positive Authenticity and Honesty. Mean what you say and do that.
4) Support the Success of others with an Abundance Attitude. There is enough in the world for everyone

3 : RESULTS

FUNDAMENTAL BELIEF: I Create Value

DEVELOPMENTAL ACTIONS

1) Be Accountable and Responsible for your Performance. Don't blame others. Be Proactive
2) Seek and Share Feedback on Performance. Especially Seek Feedback from others who are critical of you or your performance
3) Focus on learning to be a Reliable Resource to deliver Results. Come through as often as you can. Especially when others doubt your ability.
4) Deliver Customer Delight Value within and outside the Organization

4 : STRESS & PRESSURE

FUNDAMENTAL BELIEF: I am Capable and Competent

DEVELOPMENTAL ACTIONS

1) Manage Stress and Stressors. Especially become a great Time Manager
2) Encourage and Manage Productive Conflict. Seek others who think differently from you.
3) Value and Secure the Needs of Others. Be someone who looks out for others
4) Live and Lead your Core Values and Vision everyday. Be a great Ambassador for what you stand for and align your actions with your values

5 : LEAD & INFLUENCE

FUNDAMENTAL BELIEF: I Deserve to Lead

DEVELOPMENTAL ACTIONS

1) Develop Positive Leadership Temperament and Standards. Be leader YOU would like to follow
2) Influence, Ignite & Lead the Process of Change. Start small and keep growing the Challenge of Change
3) Demonstrate Purpose and Passion in Performance. Find your sweet spot.
4) Motivate and Inspire Others to Lead. Build Leaders not Followers

Keep a Journal and record your observations, feelings, and opinion every week, if possible, every day. This shall become a visual tool to see just how life is turning out as you progress practicing your reframed beliefs, through the actions you consciously and mindfully choose to act on.

Chapter Nine
UNLOCKING LIFE, EMPOWERING BELIEFS

Life is like a giant treasure chest. Waiting to be unlocked, so that the wondrous riches and treasures within are presented to the one with the key.

The strangest thing is that, while we hold the key to this amazing treasure chest, we find ourselves handcuffed and shackled to its ornate handle!

How can that be?! You may exclaim. And yet you know it's true. For while you struggle helplessly to free yourself, people with their keys come by and plunder that treasure chest, right before your very eyes!!

The key is a magical one. It represents all your prowess in life. Your knowledge, skills, capabilities, character, your hard-earned credentials, painstakingly created brand image, goals and success blueprints. But it lacks the energy which must flow to it from you. From your mind and heart.

How can that happen, when the key is carefully stowed away in your pocket? And your hands are shackled and handcuffed to your beliefs. Beliefs which are written across your heart and mind and practiced by your actions. Beliefs with cast doubt in their own proclamation. Beliefs which perform dazzling theatre, behind the curtains, while the world grows weary in their seats.

The challenge of the beliefs we nurture, drawn through the way we have been taught and have learned to grasp the "truths" of life, are that they limit our capabilities and deny success, rather than empower and access the treasures stowed away. Treasures which lie tantalizingly within sight!

The difficulty about releasing ourselves from the handcuffs and shackles of our beliefs is that we are in love with them. The restricted movement of doubt ridden, debt burdened and broke balance caution of our success strategies, and the less than mediocre payout, seems to satisfy us. As long as it is continuous across life.

Movement and mediocrity in steady abundance are gratifying! Like a slow rocking chair in perpetual motion, which rocks you forward to savor your meal and then rocks you away. Why don't we just pull our chairs to the dining table and heap the food onto our plates? Eat gracefully, but fill your plate first.

Reframing our beliefs to empower our actions allows us to unlock the goodness of life.

As you shall see in the chapter that follows our beliefs are set into the stories that we tell ourselves. The stories that are constantly running through our mind, the scripts of which we have been writing right through our lives. We now have to throw these stories away. Amending or adapting them would lead to the original story staying behind and simply being re-packaged in new covers, but with the same old script. We have to change the storyline completely.

To do this, we have to revisit our life in a powerful way, looking through the lens of the successes that we have experienced rather than the failures. Looking through what we know we can achieve rather that what we doubt. Looking through the window however will not get us into the playing field.

There is where the treasure of life lies. Amidst the jostling of lives, the shared breath of support, the dynamic vision of goals , sometimes above the tall shoulders and often through the stampeding limbs of players, partners, competitors, supporters and referees of the wonderfully enthralling game of life.

Empowering beliefs bring strength to your limbs, oxygen to your lungs, adrenaline in your blood, courage to your heart and fire the hundred billion neurons in your brain to wire them together in a joyful pursuit of the prized ball, in a game you know you have won. Just because you were there. From the previous chapter let's take a look at all those statements of developmental actions for each of the Five Fundamental Beliefs.

For each statement we shall examine what could be a Limiting

Assumption or Belief which shackles us and what could be an Empowering Assumption or Belief which can unlock our lives and the treasure chest.

REFRAMING YOUR BELIEF BLUEPRINT - Choosing Empowering Beliefs (EB) over Limiting Beliefs (LB).

Living Your Beliefs through an UNLOCKED EQ Purposed Life

1 : SELF

FUNDAMENTAL BELIEF: I am Worthy. Others are too. DEVELOPMENTAL ACTIONS

1) **Develop Significant Purpose in Life to have a more meaningful life. Set Life Goals**.

LB: There's no point in developing significant Purpose. The goal posts of life shift too rapidly. Take life as it comes.

EB: Purpose is essential to bring meaning to my life. It helps me follow and hold firmly onto the shifting goalposts. I can make life work.

2) **Develop Courage to face Adversity with more Optimism,** Ownership and Endurance. Know what it takes to see things through the rough times.LB: Adversity increases with resistance to it. Optimism obscure the truth of reality.

Just knowing what it takes does not guarantee success.

EB: Optimism, Ownership and Endurance are essential tools in my toolkit for life. I put my best efforts to using these tools and I keep getting good at using them. I know it helps me deal effectively with adversity.

3) Develop Compassion for others and the ability to Forgive yourself and others.

LB: Compassion is a sign of weakness. Forgiveness is a chink in the armour.

EB: Compassion is strength. Forgiveness builds Character

4) Develop a Change Plan to Personally Make a Difference and become an Agent of Change. Take responsibility for Change.

LB: Change Happens to me. Change is uncontrollable. Just learn to survive change.

EB: I am responsible for my life and those who need me to support them. Change is a Way of Life. I learn to thrive.

2 : OTHERS

FUNDAMENTAL BELIEF: I Support the Success of Others
DEVELOPMENTAL ACTIONS

1) **Build a Spirit of Collaboration and Support**. Not just co-operation. Collaboration is full engagement.

LB: Collaboration is a flawed strategy. It creates room for confusion, disorganization and even betrayal and harm. Stay strong and handle matters yourself. Command and Lead.

EB: Collaboration builds Trust. It is the greatest gift to teams and communities. Collaboration delivers outstanding results. I choose to collaborate.

2) **Be Trustworthy in everything. Especially little things. All the time.**

LB: I cannot force people to trust me. People can't be trusted to do the right thing regardless of what I do.

EB: Trust is a gift. I don't value a gift just by its size. Trust is a gift which must be traded. I choose to be trustworthy. I know it is always returned.

3) **Communicate with Positive Authenticity and Honesty**. Mean what you say and do that.

LB: Lies and Untruths are a part of life. Authenticity leads to unnecessary vulnerability. Nothing really works out exactly so why pretend to care.

EB: Authenticity leads to Vulnerability. Vulnerability is Strength. Visible Authenticity is the trademark of honesty. I choose to be authentic and vulnerable.

4) **Support the Success of others with an Abundance Attitude**. There is enough in the world for everyone

LB: Everyone must compete to succeed.

EB: Others need me just as I need them. Combining strengths takes full teams to the top of the mountain. The view is magnificent when it is shared.

3: RESULTS

FUNDAMENTAL BELIEF: I Create Value

DEVELOPMENTAL ACTIONS

1) **Be Accountable and Responsible for your Performance**. Don't blame others. Be Proactive

LB: Everyone who shares the benefits must share the Labours of the process. No man is an island. Others must share blame too.

EB: As a Car Owner, when driving my car or being driven in it, I remain the owner. And all that goes with that title. Life is the same. It's my car.

2) **Seek and Share Feedback on Performance**. Especially Seek Feedback from others who are critical of you or your performance

LB: Why bother about what others think ? Most people try to put you down. Others just don't care. Do what you have to do and move on.

EB: Feedback are like mirrors in life. They are valuable sources of prized information. Especially when they clearly show you what you don't expect or wish to see. I choose to listen to feedback. It's a gift I cannot refuse.

3) **Focus on learning to be a Reliable Resource to deliver Results.** Come through as often as you can. Especially when others doubt your ability.

LB: . I do what I can. Can't move mountains. Being a reliable resource to others makes them weak, inefficient and ineffective. Direct others to be self sufficient and independent

EB: I love challenges. The harder the better. Muscles develop through constant flexing and rigour. Life needs robustness and reliability. I choose to deliver every time. Just like I want my car to work every time I turn the key. And yes, there's always room for passengers. It makes my journey feel great. I always learn from the small talk too.

4) **Deliver Customer Delight Value within and outside the Organization**

LB: Delight becomes Demand. Learn to Satisfy. That's what is expected and charged for. More costs more. Profit is better than happiness

EB: Delight becomes Demand. Satisfaction is now Delight. The only way into a customer's wallet is through the heart. Internal customers wallets are filled with support, time, encouragement and profit flows from this. I choose to Delight!

4 : STRESS & PRESSURE

FUNDAMENTAL BELIEF : I am Capable and Competent

DEVELOPMENTAL ACTIONS

1) **Manage Stress and Stressors. Especially become a great Time Manager**

LB: Time can never be managed. It always is about Power. The more powerful you are, the more time becomes irrelevant.

EB: Time is about Energy. Manage your Energy and you can Manage Time. It never fails and always improves.

2) **Encourage and Manage Productive Conflict**. Seek others who think differently from you.

LB: Life is full of unwanted conflict. Why seek it. It finds you anyway! Thinking differently is the cause of poor and delayed decision making. Crush conflict or pay the price!

EB: Conflict is the secret to great decisions, choices and results. Many minds are powerful when they find ways to work together like a jigsaw puzzle. Different pieces fit together without losing identity. I choose to engage in conflict to celebrate what others think, feel and perceive.

3) **Value and Secure the Needs of Others.** Be someone who looks out for others

LB: I am not a Safekeeper of other peoples' valuables. Who is looking after me?

EB: People may or not remember and return the help they receive. When it's unconditional, it strikes a deep chord. That's always returned. Stephen Covey called it Emotional Bank Accounting.in his famed book "7 Habits of Highly Effective People"

4) **Live and Lead your Core Values and Vision everyday**. Be a great Ambassador for what you stand for and align your actions with your values

LB: Ambassadors get Assassinated. An ambassador is a diplomat. Diplomats hedge their bets. Learn to Align with what's valuable to your career vision.

EB: Walk the Talk. It matters. Ambassadors become Presidents too.

5: LEAD & INFLUENCE

FUNDAMENTAL BELIEF: I Deserve to Lead

DEVELOPMENTAL ACTIONS

1) **Develop Positive Leadership Temperament and Standards.** Be leader YOU would like to follow

LB: Leaders need to Control. Control can't always be Positive. Man up. Kick Ass.

EB: A Resonant Leader resonates with minds and hearts. Tough love is still love. Celebrating the Leader in me wins over Admiration of the Leader in me.

2) **Influence, Ignite & Lead the Process of Change**. Start small and keep growing the Challenge of Change

LB: Let Change arrive first. You can't outsmart change before you know what it is.

EB: Anticipating Change is best when you trigger it. Pro-action is the trigger.

3) **Demonstrate Purpose and Passion in Performance.** Find your sweet spot.

LB: Purpose and Passion are hard uncomfortable places. Together they are devastating. What if things go wrong? What a waste of effort and energy!

EB: Purpose and Passion offer direction and drive. It's like a driving a super car with a tank full of gas and GPS, while your favorite music plays. Rock your journey! Give me P&P any day! Wherever I go, my P&P shall follow through.

4) **Motivate and Inspire Others to Lead. Build Leaders not Followers**

LB: Leaders need Followers. What's the point of being a Leader without followers?!

EB: Creating Strong Competent Leadership is about lifting people to be better than they think they can. Then letting them take ownership. What's better than that?!

Well, that does provide you with a pretty good idea how Limiting Beliefs can limit and deny you success. Empowering Beliefs on the other hand release and unlock the shackles and handcuffs. Life itself is Unlocked!

You would be well advised to keep a Journal and record your observations, feelings, and opinion every week, if possible,

I BELIEVE

every day. This shall become a visual tool to see just how life is turning out as you progress practicing your reframed beliefs, through the actions you consciously and mindfully choose to act on.

Chapter Ten
CHANNELING THE POWER OF BELIEFS

This is where our Beliefs not only come to life, but become life itself.

Many of us are struggling with the burden of our beliefs. To make them count often ends with our beliefs trapping us rather than releasing us to our powerful lives.

In my book Flawed Yet Precious, I have written about how the lens which we look through and critically examine, interpret and judge life, is about the Flaws in life. We try hard to scrub the stains, darn the rips, add embroidery to, tuck in the loosened stitching and recreate as much as possible, the faded fabric of life, to appear Precious. Because we prefer to present the Precious and hide the Flaws.

Yet what if it were the Flaws which make the jewel Precious, the worn threads which provide comfort to make the fabric Precious!

What if life needs the Flaws in order to be Precious? Our belief system would need a bit of work to channel the power of our beliefs through the flaws, to the precious.

I BELIEVE

I wish to take this further through my own journey through my beliefs as they matured through the flaws and turned Precious.

Some years ago, as part of my own coaching journey as a professional life and executive coach, I was asked by my own coach to write 10 Significant Lessons of Life.

These turned out to be my own 10 Beliefs of Life. Allow me to share these with you. Here they are :

1. I am capable of rising to the top of anything I choose to do or choose to be. But remember it gets lonely at the top.
2. Life has opportunities but it takes frustration and often bitterness with the present situation to see them and then choose to change
3. Change is Vital. Change is ugly too.
4. Colleagues are important to have, to reflect on ideas together and share plans. Be careful with what you disclose.
5. Not everyone is loyal. Betrayal is a given.
6. Some decisions need a scary leap of faith. Use a safety net.
7. I need someone who can be an anchor in my life, but I need to be in charge of the ship.
8. Reinvention is the name of the game. Nothing works the way you first used it.
9. Consistency is important but it could block creativity.

10. Life is a series of challenging experiments. Try to survive each one and thrive from the experiences that they generate.

This seemed pretty good, but as you will notice, these powerful beliefs are embedded with hesitant, negative, contradictory, misaligned words which derail the energy and power train from the tracks of a truly great life. These are part of old stories; from the old book of life I had been diligently writing into my subconscious mind. And now they were here, dancing in the sunshine of my "wisdom".

So, I decided to define Life in short, to get to my core belief. And what I saw was good. But was it good enough to write my new story in a new book of life? We shall see.

Here is my core belief about life:

Life is a gigantic, ginormous canvass of lived experiences, with people to love, places to discover, power to influence and lead and to create a significant legacy for the future.

Which led to answering this question. The answer to which revealed my Fundamental Belief. A belief which actually drove my Core Beliefs.

I BELIEVE
The Question: What Am I Here For?

My Answer and Fundamental Belief:

I am here to set up the foundation for the future of my family and what I wish the world to be.

To find my own true purpose and help others find theirs. To make my name a true "Brand" to live way beyond my life.

Wonderful, isn't it ? Well, sort of.

With such a powerful, rigid and absolute statement of my fundamental belief, where would it leave me in the downturn of times, when none of these statements worked? While nothing is permanent, my fundamental belief which was my engine of energy would drain it away completely. My powerful positive fundamental belief was all about the end result and not about the journey. The journey is where life is lived. So if a fundamental belief cannot power the journey, it may not be true at the end too!

At this point, I simply HAD to ask myself a really tough question.

WHAT IS THE PRICE I AM PAYING FOR REPLAYING OLD FAULTY STORIES?

Here is what I realized.

1. I cannot fully live my current story because I cannot see past my old story
2. I deal with regret rather that promise
3. I feel small and vulnerable
4. I feel others can't count on me to provide the life we deserve
5. I am not growing the Brand I created, by diverting attention and focus to old stories.

Naturally, this discovery unnerved me quite a bit. In order to regain composure, I decided to make a small list of what I was thankful and grateful for, before the clouds of self-doubt rolled in permanently like a perpetual fog.

And this is what it was and still is.

MY CORE GRATITUDE LIST

What I am thankful and grateful for.

1. My Family
2. My Talents and skills
3. My Social Status
4. My Nature of Generosity and Trust (my old story put this into the bad box of being taken advantage of)

5. My Type of Work as a Consultant (Old Story was about irregularity of business and unfair bargains)
6. My Own Private Exclusive Office Space
7. My Friends who believe in me
8. My Privileged Lifestyle
9. My Access to Resources - Mechanisms and People who literally support my life.
10. My Clients- past, present and those to come; everyone I have met or engaged with for business, across all parts of my multifold career.

It became clear that I needed to lower an anchor to keep my boat steady and moored to a sense of abundance and joy. So I decided to make a few promises to myself. Three Promises.

Take a look.

My 3 PROMISES to me.

1. I choose to celebrate who I am, as I am blessed, I am loved, I am gifted and I am worthy of all of these and of immense success
2. I choose to be grateful for all and any work I do. Regardless of what it pays or even who knows about it.
3. To always honour and cherish my family, my friends and all those with whom I have shared moments of my life with. Especially to do this in moments when I am not the best version of myself.

Days of reflection followed. I was slowly getting around the almost derailing discoveries to a point of reset.

My old stories had to end being the voice in my head. I decided to write my new story. This may inspire you to write yours too. In fact, I am sure it shall.

Here are the beliefs of my new story. And this helps me everyday today. It helped me write 8 books in 7 months across the global pandemic lockdown, from April 2020 to October 2020.

This is my 9th book.

MY NEW STORY

Everyday has something new to learn and do. Every moment is an experiment

Success is how I feel about myself and why I matter. I see the future I create regardless of the resources.

What I need to deliver my dream, I already have but may not know I do.

I discover everyday my latent strengths and talents, which unfailingly present themselves to me.

I journey with hope, onwards and forward, to each new day and each new opportunity and express myself in many ways.

I BELIEVE

I make the time every day to identify and use my talents. I choose to leave the stories of my past to my past. That book is complete. It was well written, a best seller. It has my gratitude.

I now script my new story, one which acknowledges everyday I live and celebrates the life I create as I live.

The book I write today, is not the book I wrote yesterday. Nor is it the book I wish I wrote yesterday.

I do what I can do.

I accept the journey to my goals.

I believe in my journey.

My journey redeems my belief in me.

I always give the journey of life my best shot. It's what I do anyway

I Can Always Count on Me!

To keep this new book open and valid, I had to do more than just write it. I needed to believe in it, every day. The best way to do this, was to Affirm my Beliefs. Through daily affirmations, which on reading each morning would become my prayer to the Universe. One which would be returned to me.

MY AFFIRMATIONS OF LIFE

I am grateful for all the goodness in my life and all that is on its way to me.

I am grateful for the abundance that is flowing into my life.

I am making lots of money doing what I love.

I now manifest the magical life I have imagined.

I believe in my skills and my abilities.

People respect and pay me handsomely for my work.

Success, money and happiness come easily to me.

Every day in every way I receive more and more abundantly

I can afford anything I want in life.

I am a magnet for money and prosperity is drawn to me.

I deserve to be well paid for my skills and knowledge.

I am wealthy and prosperous in all areas of my life.

I am receiving all the wealth that the universe has for me.

I am open to receive infinite blessings from the universe.

I am a magnet for divine abundance in the form of money, health and happiness.

I BELIEVE

I am attracting unconditional love, abundance, high vibrational experiences and sacred connections.

I am whole, I am perfect, I am strong, I am powerful, I am loving, I am harmonious, I am happy, I am rich.

I release past anger and hurts and fill myself with serenity and peaceful thoughts.

I am attracting powerful positive and healthy people into my life.

The universe is filled with endless opportunities for me.

I can do anything and everything I choose to put my mind to.

I excel in all that I do and success comes easily to me.

I allow my passion to become my purpose and profession.

Things are always working out for me.

I am the architect of my life. I build my own Foundation and I choose my own bricks

SUMMARY
PUTTING BELIEFS INTO PLAY

Reading this book would have either added to your library of information or brought in new insight into life. Your life.

Either way, now that you are nearly at the end of this book, perhaps it is a good thing to lean back close your eyes, and open your mind. Let your thoughts travel across the chapters of this book and what the words have described to you. Pictures they have drawn. Visuals etched into your mind, connecting with the images you already have and scan furiously every moment, sometime consciously, but more often than not, unconsciously.

Allow me to led you into a "dream sequence". Read this first, then close your eyes and imagine it. Allow your creative mind the permission to create images, sounds, aromas, touch, feelings and sensations to make this as delightfully real as possible.

Think you are at the Theatre watching an acclaimed play "A Magnificent Life". You look at the colourful brochure and excitedly stuff it into your pocket or handbag. This play has been acclaimed the world over and here you are to see it. Finally. In premium seats, close up to the stage! And it cost you a fair bit of money. Which you paid happily!

Ah the curtains are being lifted. The stage is dark. A spotlight turns on. The lead actor appears on stage. Looking across every inch of the stage for something. What is being searched for? You know the answer already. Guess what it is!

The play A Magnificent Life begins with Man's Search for the Magnificence of Life !

The Acts of the play are announced. There is a sense of great familiarity with them. You long to look at the brochure you stuffed away, but the theatre is dark, and using your mobile light is forbidden.

You settle back into your seat and decide to be present to the unfolding scenes.

ACT 1 OBSERVING OUR WORLD

The actors go through each part of the stage, crawling, walking, running around, bumping into people and objects. The amazing thing you observe is that each of them have notebooks in which they are constantly making notes. They keep leafing back and forth across their notebooks. Sometimes they sit down perplexed, sometimes they indicate they have captured something wonderful, sometimes they jump back in terror, running off the stage, then reappearing very timidly and tentatively. Still holding their notebooks and waving them in some sort of argument as proof of something special. Quite a pantomime! You can't help laughing, but find it quite a lot like what you do and see others do too.

ACT 2 INTERACTING WITH THE WORLD WE OBSERVE

This gets even more interesting. The actors now get involved with the stage props and other actors. They experiment with pushing, prodding, feeling, smelling, embracing first just a little, then with increasing vigour, frequency and abandon.

Naturally, in whatever they do, they get pushback actions for the other people. The props just rock around helpless, sometimes falling over with a resounding thud, startling the actors, who quickly restore them to their original positions, furtively looking around to check who has observed that happen.

This has you and others in the audience laughing out loudly. Tears streaming from the eyes. Yet through it all, these ring several bells about your own life. You start seeing many similarities. The script writer must have quite a similar like to you, you begin to think.

And yes, the notebooks are still there. Though actors now keep taking breaks to write their notes before get back into action. Hmmm, that's interesting.

ACT 3 OPINIONS, JUDGEMENTS, BELIEFS, INTERPRETATIONS

This is the last Act before the break. You feel something significant is about to happen. Something which shall serve to influence the conversations over coffee and sandwiches in the break

The dark stage brightens.

Actors are now engaged in various part of their lives. Family, School, College, Workplace, Teams, Marriage, Own Family, Getting Older, Kids growing up, Jobs being lost, Finance being hard to manage, Kids getting Married, New Career, Change in location, New Country of residence, Strange New Cultures, Adjusting to Kids' Lives and Needs, Becoming Grandparents, Getting Outdated, Getting Sick, Losing a Partner, Dying.

Sob ! Tears in every eye in the audience. Silence. Someone is crying. On gosh. It's you.

Mercifully it is time for the first break.

ACT 4 BELIEF BASES

Old age wisdom. Advice for life. Kids and family around the fireplace. Stories are told about the truths of life, as they were learned. Some in time to act on, some in time to pass on. They include these 4 Belief Bases which describe the world in what appears to be meaningful, but largely untested ways.

There are explanations that make wonderful stories about each one. About Empowering beliefs which deliver a better

94

life and Limiting Beliefs which led to a bitter life. Or that is how it is described by the actors. You make a note to check on this yourself. Better versus Bitter.

Belief Base #1
BELIEFS ABOUT THE WORLD
Belief Base # 2
BELIEFS ABOUT LIFE & LIVING
Belief Base #3
BELIEFS ABOUT SELF
Belief Base # 4
BELIEFS ABOUT THE FUTURE

How interesting! You remark to yourself. All these beliefs, across the Four Bases; about the World, about Life and Living, about Self and about the Future; as recounted on stage, are so similar to the ones you hold.

Yet now that they are being announced, discussed and debated under the spotlight and elevated on a stage, some of these beliefs seem to ring quite hollow. Must reflect on these later, you make another mental note.

Whew! This is turning out to be a long yet absorbing play! No wonder it has received such rave reviews.

ACT 5 ACTING ON BELIEFS – CHOICES, DECISIONS, ACTIONS. FUELED BY EMPOWERING BELIEFS WHICH UNLOCK LIFE

Now the stage is divided into 5 areas. They have big banners proclaiming: SELF, OTHERS, RESULTS, STRESS & PRESSURE, LEAD & INFLUENCE. The spotlight focuses on one area at a time. The others are in darkness.

The stories continue with tremendous and vivid vitality. Bringing to life, the wise lessons of the wise and learned people you saw in Act 4

Sometimes a second and even a third and fourth spotlight suddenly turn on to beam into the other dark areas of the stage. That's when you realize how interconnected these areas are! You feel like requesting the stage manager to turn on all 5 spotlights at the same time! And Hallelujah! They all are turned on!

1: SELF

FUNDAMENTAL BELIEF: I am Worthy. Others are too.

2: OTHERS

FUNDAMENTAL BELIEF: I Support the Success of Others

3 : RESULTS

FUNDAMENTAL BELIEF: I Create Value

4 : STRESS & PRESSURE

FUNDAMENTAL BELIEF: I am Capable and Competent

5 : LEAD & INFLUENCE

FUNDAMENTAL BELIEF: I Deserve to Lead

Aha! That makes so much sense now!

Why were these simple things not known earlier to these actors, you wonder? You make a mental note to write to the script writer.

Thankfully another break is announced at the end of Act 5

Just the Concluding Act remains. That must be really special.

Time for Act 6. You see uniformed ushers from the play, amidst the audience, selecting people from the audience to follow them. What's up, you wonder! Suddenly you feel someone tap your shoulder politely. It's an Usher. What does he want? He's asking you to follow him. Curiosity gets the better of you. The heart pumps a bit faster. Your pulse quickens. Adrenaline starts surging.

CONCLUDING ACT 6 CHANNELING THE POWER OF BELIEFS

This is a Six Act Play. Even Shakespearean Dramas are Five Act Plays. There must be a surprise in store for Act 6!! In growing excitement and wonder, you hurry to the back of the stage and meet the play management staff. They greet you with great admiration and appreciation. Another 10 to 12 people also selected from the audience are here too. You look over at them. What a surprise. You know each one of them. Very well in fact. You realize they are from different parts of your life.

Still quite puzzled, you ask the Play Managers why you have been called! What they say, shocks you!

You and the others have been called, because……

All of you are the script writers of the Play. Each Play for every show, in every part of the world, having a different set of writers. Operating withing the overall design of the Play. That's Just Like Life, you realize! And you are right.

You hurriedly pull out the Play Brochure, the one you stuffed away. Looking at it, you are thrilled to see your name written clearly as one of the twelve scriptwriters of this show's Play!

Now that you know this, you look for Act 6 and what it is about! Well. Well.. what do you read?

Take a guess before reading ahead!

Aha!!!

It says: The Scriptwriters shall deliver an impromptu Improv Show, on the Power of Beliefs in their Lives and how they influenced, inspired and ignited their individual and collective lives!

The stage darkens. Lights grow bright gradually. The Stage is aglow! Audience cheer! You set your life into new motion. The stage whirls around you. Life is alive and alight. Somewhere in time, the curtain falls. You can hear the audience applauding like rolls of thunder. The curtain rises. Everyone is on their feet. Strobe lights flash. The stage is enveloped in golden ticker tape showers. Dramatic music plays!

In a quiet place in your mind, you make a promise to yourself. To journal this night. In as much detail as you can recall. Then add your insights to it. That would make this a great memory. And a great memoir. A legacy you must leave.

CONCLUDING REFLECTIONS
By the Author Dexter John Valles

This book has been a journey for me. Across the fundamentals of my own assumptions, beliefs, values and emotions. I have shared with you how I traversed across the stories of my life. Writing page after page, chapter upon chapter and volume after volume about all I believed that life had taught me. Beliefs I enshrined, Values I venerated and Emotional tides I swam with, to reach the shores of success. And I did.

As an MBA from an institute of repute, and as a student of some standing, I launched myself into a job in international business, that seemed to suit my dreams in such a magical way. I travelled tirelessly across the world setting up markets and forging relationships which delivered big business in the most testing of times. I believed with all my heart, that this was it. I had truly made it. Racing across Performance milestones, setting benchmarks, I was out performing my own expectations.

Yet suddenly at the zenith of my prowess, the celebration of that glorious success faded away. I realized that something had to change. Everything I believed to be true for me, wasn't as true anymore.

I believed in highly qualified job security and growth in a big brand corporate house. I believed in doing the best job, even if it wasn't a true fit. You see, my success story involved me exporting electrical engineering products, from a renowned electrical engineering company in India. And I wasn't an engineer. I was and am a Science graduate, specialized in Chemistry. With an MBA Degree in Marketing Management. Yet here I was, powered by my beliefs, shining my light through a job that wasn't really part of my original dream job, nor was I actually truly meant to do it.

My belief engine was sputtering, despite my career locomotive ploughing on gleaming tracks through the landscape of my life! Oddly enough it left me wondering if that was really enough.

I had to challenge every belief in my box, to leave my job at the very pinnacle of success and launch myself outside my old belief system and stop writing my old story in new books. I needed a new story, in a new book of reframed and recast beliefs.

Working through the prejudices and biases in my own mental framework, a natural outcome of prolonged exposure to my belief system, I decided that my newly recalibrated belief system had to be one based on more visible evidence, grown and guided by clarified values and emotions, aligned to my deeper life purpose.

I BELIEVE

It was okay to pause in the midst of traffic to check my map.

Visiting my core beliefs, I realized that they actually pointed to the life I now lead. Far different from the one I had and even in quite another direction. As a Consultant in the field of behavioural science, human resource management, learning and development and life & executive coaching.

Somehow, I didn't listen to those protesting voices of my values and emotions, shrieking their objection to my early career choices and actions. I did use different beliefs to deliver outstanding results, though the limiting beliefs of my choice of Passion blindfolded my vision and golden handcuffed me to a career, I finally abandoned at the age of 32.

At 55 today, I know that my belief system has found it's true voice.

Empowering beliefs allow me to listen more. And during this lockdown I have listened closely to the voice of my soul. That's where our truths go to build their homes, procreate, have families and proliferate.

The choices grow when you affirm your beliefs with positive power, unshackle and unlock life to run with great abandon in the garden of your dreams, dance with your darkest emotions, add sparkle to your values, zing to your goals, and zest to your quest for an enchanted life.

Just knowing that you can choose to follow your heart right into the deepest valley of your life and chase after it to the top of the mountains, is such a liberating feeling of freedom.

Freedom to be the best you can ever be, way beyond the limits and boundaries of claustrophobic beliefs born and raised in the shadow of your soul and barely ignited by the flame of your spirit.

May this book of beliefs show you the way to those magnificent parts of your life, you don't yet dare to dream.

This book is part of that dream. So are the eight I wrote before this.

Because, I BELIEVE!

A CASE STUDY

As I have often felt, concepts are best understood when they reflect in the turmoil of life. Here, caught in the crosshairs of reality, we are both participants as well as witnesses to the chaos and complexity of circumstances in their most mesmerizing forms.

Hypnotic enough, for us to let go of all our learning and understanding of the possibilities and choices we have by reframing this reality through the lenses of the higher self. Instead, we get to "work" with the skills and knowledge we have readily at hand, practiced to perfection.

Perfection in an imagined sense of effectiveness. And usually set in our old comfortable beliefs. Even when they actually result in a lot of discomfort. They are what we fall back on, because they are always available. Unless we learn to practice them away.

This case study is about a curious mix of people, doing just that. In the context of organizational life. You are allowed to smile unabashedly as you recognize quite a few of them in your own life! Maybe one of them could be coloured with shades of your very own life too!

KEEP THESE QUESTIONS IN MIND WHILE READING THROUGH THE PROFILES AND STORIES OF THE PERSONNEL WORKING AT BIOCOSMIC CORPORATION

QUESTIONS FOR YOUR REFLECTION

1. What do you think are the Beliefs of each of these people? Choose around 12 people to study in more detail.
2. What kind of Beliefs do they hold or practice – Limiting or Empowering?
3. What do you recommend each one of them does to make their relationships work? How do you feel it will it impact the business?
4. What change is required to their Beliefs to result into more effective and desirable behaviour and their consequences?
5. Could you write a Key New Belief for each one?

It does not really matter how accurate you are with your answers. Behaviour is hardly based on accuracy of thought. It is important and useful though for you to reflect and see the choices available, when beliefs shift.
That's when the magic begins!

A Peek into Life at

BIOCOSMIC CORPORATION

Company Profile: Major Player in the Personal Care Products Industry. Manufacturing and selling Skin Care, Hair Care and Personal Grooming Products for Women and Men.

Company Management: Professional management, part of a multi-domestic foreign MNC, with local staffing.

Business Scale: Right across the Product Range, but mainly in Urban Markets

Reputation in the Market: Good, but could improve considerably. Seen as confused about product positioning and consistency of image. Some brands from the same stable appear to be openly and fiercely competitively poised against each other. Too many quick product introductions and sudden withdrawals, points to inadequate market research and shallow marketing / business strategy. Dealers and distributors feel distanced from the company's plans and no longer share the earlier sense of identity, involvement and bonding. This is thought to be largely due to the new breed of young highly qualified management inducted over the last 2 years who are seen as working with major disconnects with the earlier experienced but not as professionally qualified managers

Major Business Issues: Increasing the Business Volume, Range and Geographical Coverage. Managing the threat from local manufactures that are re-positioning and aggressively marketing products in strategic alliances with International brands to suit different needs across different target customer levels

Major Internal Issues: A team that is fragmented in its ways of working, a lack of Clear Common Vision and an unhealthy competition between peers and brand product lines. A general level of paranoia within the business groups that is heading towards breakdown in even basic communication and common courtesies. Formation of cliques and power broking.

BIOCOSMIC - PEOPLE PROFILE

Rakesh Dutta, CEO
The BOSS – All 4 General Managers report to him
Self assured dynamic progressive, result driven, high profile track record, Big picture person, Clear vision. Believes that competent individuals should not be constrained by incompetent teams or team leaders. Promotes an open door policy.

Janet Pinto, Executive Secretary
Executive Assistant to The BOSS – She is the defacto Second in Command
Efficient, grown through the ranks, store house of information, guarded friendliness, keeps confidences, very reliable and dependable, reserved demeanor

Prasad Gokhale, General Manager – Sales
MBA, Tier 1 Institute, 39years old
Head of Sales – All Regional Sales Manages directly report to him
Quiet, Soft spoken, Introspective, Deeply analytical, Thrives on data, often leading to "near-paralysis-by-analysis". More often than not viewed as indecisive and lacking the appropriate high powered leadership qualities. Mild mannered, and often given to consensus driven management of issues, he is seen as submissive. Some subordinates therefore feel a lack of support in higher-pitched-and –politicked matters escalated to his level.

As opposed to being strident and assertive, a quality found in such positions, Prasad is usually patient and placatory. Quick decisions are considered to be too risky, so Prasad takes his time.

Rajeev – Regional Sales Manager – West
MBA, Tier 2 Institute, 25years old
Over confident, Casual business approach, More talk than action, tends to shift blame to market vagaries or management strategy. Openly opposes the GM- Sales in open forums. Has a chip on the shoulder. Believes his Tier 2 Premier MBA Institute is superior to the Tier 1 Institutes . Can be very annoying and considered to be the local loudmouth.

Sanjay – Regional Sales Manager – North
MBA, Tier 3 Institute, 27years old
Aggressive, Flashy, Fast and smooth talker, Achiever. Believes he is the best successor for GM- Sales. Curries favor with Prasad GM- Sales covertly but s quick to point out his own achievements to Rakesh Dutta – CEO at any available opportunity . Overtly talkative and friendly, but not very receptive to share free time / advice when his own aims and objectives are not in focus.

Debasis- Regional Sales Manager – East
MBA, Tier 1 Institute, 28years old
Intellectual but laid back, a good analyst but not interested in aggressively promoting strategic recommendations to improve business, content with incremental performance. Often the target of Rajeev's anti Tier1 Institute jokes. Does not take his performance appraisal seriously, and does not feel the need to discuss his personal views / issues with anyone. Is fast becoming an "intellectual recluse" and is often derisively called "The Bengal Pussycat"

Krishnan – Regional Sales Manager- South
MBA, Tier 2 Institute, 30years old
Generates good ideas but not articulate, unable to present his case to GM- Sales , highly frustrated and de motivated. Tends to set low targets due to this , generally considered to be an underachiever , Believes that Sanjeev Mathur GM –Mktg would be better as GM –Sales and therefore takes his troubles to the willing ears of Sanjeev. Came close to being sacked over his poor performance. Has become very guarded about his views and tends to stay to himself. Takes criticism as a pinch of salt.

Sanjeev Mathur, General Manager Marketing

Masters Degree in Commerce, 36years old

Head of Marketing – All Segment Managers Report to him Ambitious, Aggressive business strategist, tireless worker, high on process orientation with high hands- on management approach, keen eye for detail – tends to nitpick, very demanding on subordinates and channel partners. Cannot take criticism and is very quick to suppress any emerging leader. Suffers from a great fear that a professional/MBA may stake claim to his job versus his M.Com qualification. Does not actively participate in off-the-job events/functions and is generally seen as unsociable.

Kalpana, Segment Manager – Hair Care
Post Graduate, Mass Communication; 35years old

Is considered the natural successor to the post of GM- MKtg. However is often the target of Sanjeev's criticism. She is soft spoken good at her job but not assertive. Has recently experienced severe team trauma with Sonali openly opposing her and going over her head directly to a receptive Sanjeev

Sonali, Product Manager- ALLURE
MBA, Tier 2 Institute, 28years old

Reports to Kalpana

Ambitious, Highly aggressive, often abrasive, Manipulative and shrewd judge of people. Considers other business SM's & PM's as rivals and even in her own group does not share information with Amit. Very secretive and possessive of the Allure brand success of which she believes is due to her. Can be very "bitchy" and spiteful. Tries to boss Amit due to her longer experience at Biocosmic and University MBA ranking

Amit, Product Manager - CZAR
MBA – Tier 2 Institute, 26years old
Reports to Kalpana
Friendly and loyal to Kalpana, good at his job, open to criticism and willing to discuss issues openly. Believes that team leaders should be given a chance to lead, and considers Sonali an over ambitious troublemaker. Has even tried approaching her with his feelings on improving team cohesiveness, but with little success. Likes to be involved with the team and the business. Is generally considered to be a nice guy, a good buddy to hang out with.

Rekha, Segment Manager (Skincare)
MBA- 3 Years Part Time Course, 32years old
Balanced , mature , good delegator and people developer, aware of her strengths and weakness and is open to feedback. Shares an open , equal an honest working relationship with her PM Amit. Technically competent and confident, her strategy is based on collaboration and trust. She cannot understand why other team cannot get along well and has often tried to counsel warring colleagues resulting in her and her PM being ostracized from the other teams. However, she prefers to work thing out herself rather than escalate issues which she feels is immature and burdens seniors with unnecessary dilemmas

Arun, Product Manager – GOLITE
MBA, Tier 2 Institute, 26years old
Reports to Rekha
Shares a warm relationship with his boss and is a good friend to Amit. Just like his boss he is open to sharing information and discussing issues rather than jumping to conclusions. Despite the negative approach of other teams, Arun often goes out of the way to share information and include others in his business strategy meetings. He tries hard to bring convergence of the resources, and believes that he will succeed despite the current obstacles. He is know to be almost magically gifted with the ability to find the right people or the right resources at the right time and is gaining the reputation of being Mr. Fix – It

Aditya, Segment Manager (Personal Grooming)
MBA, Tier 1 Institute, 31years old
Is highly qualified and a gold medalist from XLRI. Has designs on the post of GM-Marketing, however needs a few more years to be considered mature for the job. Is unhappy with the product range he is handling and believes it lies outside the core-competencies of the company and is really peripheral to the main line of products. He is critical over the lack of support in terms of resources being allocated to this product segment esp. in view of the undifferentiated/me-too product offering to a buying segment that largely displays a low-involvement, brand-switching buying behaviour. However is keen not to get on the wrong side of Sanjeev and is often supportive of Sanjeev's strategies in the boardroom, while being most critical within his team. As a result is not trusted a lot by his team, and is often kept out of informal team meetings and team get-togethers , much to

his disappointment. Cannot take criticism no matter how mild, therefore is often left alone.

Vidya, Product Manager – ULTRA FAB
MBA, Tier 2 Institute, 25years old
Reports to Aditya

Looks upto Sonali as a role model. Consequently she has also distanced herself from Amit, Arun and Kalpana. Seeks to showcase her achievements at every possible opportunity directly to Sanjeev Mathur, believing that she will be made the next Segment Manager –Personal Grooming, as she has come across information that Aditya is looking out for a job elsewhere. Is hardly experienced but is a glib talker and has a sharp and very agile mind. Is extremely good at her work but refuses to give credit to her team mate Mohan, who was largely responsible for her induction training and on the job mentoring in the first 6 months. Is very inquisitive about others plans and analysis of business and office politics, but is very quick to deflect queries about her own views. Can often be rude and insensitive to people's feelings. Believes that business success is largely based on high risk to get high returns tends to throw caution to the wind quite often. It is left to Mohan to bail her out of business cul-de-sacs, though this is rewarded with ballistic reprimands to stop interfering rather than even quiet appreciation. Gets hurt at the mildest confrontation / conflict and sulks in silence for days thereafter.

Mohan, Product Manager - MACHISMO
MBA, Tier 3 Institute, 30years old
Reports to Aditya
Is the most experienced PM and is also the most matured. Is viewed by most as stable and self-assured and a good team player. Is often seen encouraging people including Vidya and Sonali when things are going contrary to plan, and offers constructive advice. Is not concerned by the office politics and distances himself from gossip and clique formation. Maintains an open communication style withal SMs and PMs and is very supportive of his SM Aditya, although he often seeks time to share his thoughts with Aditya on strategy and business plans. He is not shy to offer critical but constructive advice to Aditya, and volunteers to shoulder additional responsibility if only to prove his own business convictions. Is admired by Amit and Arun and even by Sonali, although she would never admit it openly. Yet of late she has been seeking advice from him in difficult business situations, and has found his advice to be impartial and sound.

Madhu Rege, General Manager – Finance
Chartered Accountant, Company Secretary, 45years old
Genius with figures, a good business analyst and has often proved to be invaluable to the CEO in recharting business direction and growth. Openly critical about flashy sales & marketing strategies that do not bring in enough revenue. Has been involved in head-on conflict with Sanjeev Mathur in the process. Is very clear and articulate about what he feels is his role in the business and refuses to be relegated

to the role of a glorified accountant. Is a good leader and is highly respected by his team including Supriya

Supriya, Manager – Legal
University Graduate in Arts & Humanities, Law Post Graduate
Reports to Madhu Rege
Quiet and efficient. Very good at her job. Offers her point of view very clearly and then withdraws. Does not demand compliance even if the business decision is contrary to her advice, but indicates the consequences of running the risks involved. Clearly she has defined her role and scope. Has a fine eye for detail, coupled with her legal acumen, has often saved the company a lot of expense and embarrassment. Is friendly and accessible at work, but does not like the social spotlight, so stays away from office parties and celebrations and is often considered introverted.

Vipul Vyas, General Manager -Operations
Graduate Engineer, Tier 1 Institute, 50years old
Quiet, stable, straight forward. Minds his own business, Quality focused, does not succumb to undue Marketing pressures but willing to examine product quality, complaints and suggestions on new products / improvements

PRODUCT PORTFOLIO

HAIRCARE Kalpana		SKINCARE Rekha	PERSONAL GROOMING Aditya	
CZAR	ALLURE	GLOLITE	ULTRA FAB	MACHISMO
Amit	Sonali	Arun	Vidya	Mohan
Young college / working men	Young college / working women / housewives		Young college / working / professional women Young college / working / professional men	
18- 38 years	18- 48 years	18- 58 years	18- 58 years	18- 58 years
Shampoos, Conditioners, Hair creams, Hair gels, Hair color products	Shampoos, Conditioners, Non sticky hair oil Detangling hair care, Hair color products	Face Masks, Creams, Scrubs, Bleaches, Hair removers	Deodorants sprays and roll-ons	Deodorant sprays, After shaves, Colognes

PRODUCT PORTFOLIO – BUSINESS POSITION

HAIRCARE Kalpana		SKINCARE Rekha	PERSONAL GROOMING Aditya	
ALLURE	CZAR	GLOLITE	ULTRA FAB	MACHISMO
Sonali	Amit	Arun	Vidya	Mohan
SALES PERFORMANCE OVER LAST YR*				
Stagnant	Marginal increase 5%	Grown by 40%	Grown by 10%	Marginal increase 5%
REGIONAL PERFORMANCE* NORTH, SOUTH, EAST, WEST				
NORTH Up by 25%	NORTH Up by 20%	NORTH Up by 15%	NORTH Up by 5%	NORTH Up by 10%
SOUTH Down by 15%	SOUTH Stagnant	SOUTH Up by 10%	SOUTH Stagnant	SOUTH Down by 5%
EAST Down by 15%	EAST Up by 5%	EAST Up by 20%	EAST Stagnant	EAST Stagnant
WEST Up by 10%	WEST Down by 10%	WEST stagnant	WEST Up by 10%	WEST Up by 10%

* OVER CORRESPONDING PERIOD LAST YEAR

ADDITIONAL NOTES

Some common definitions and descriptions of key words used in this book.

Source : The World Wide Web (various)

BELIEFS

Beliefs are the convictions that we generally hold to be true, usually without actual proof or evidence and are basically assumptions that we make about ourselves, other in the world and how we expect things to be. Beliefs are about how we think things really are, what we think is really true and what therefore expect as likely consequences that will follow from our behavior.

Our beliefs grow from what we see, hear, experience, read and think about. From these things we develop an opinion that we hold to be true and unmovable at that time. Additionally, they can be Empowering Beliefs, which are related to excellence and how it could be achieved, or Limiting Beliefs, where your behavior is not what you want, but you think you cannot change it.

VALUES

Values are beliefs about what a desirable is or a good (honesty) and what an undesirable is or a bad (e.g., dishonesty). Assumptions: Assumptions are beliefs that are regarded as so valuable and obviously correct that they are taken for granted and rarely examined or questioned.

ASSUMPTIONS

An "Assumption" is where you believe something to be true, but it is yet unproven while a "belief" is something you are certain is true. However, our beliefs may, in fact, be assumptions that are in the end false

How Our Beliefs Determine Life

AFFIRMATIONS

Affirmations are powerful because they have an effect on both the conscious and subconscious mind. Real change begins in the subconscious, for that's where we can change beliefs that are no longer serving us. By doing this we create room to bring in beliefs that support us.

Affirmations are used to reprogram the subconscious mind to believe certain things about ourselves or about the world and our place within it, in turn helping us create the reality we want.

A Note about this Book

This book does not in any way purport to promote, support or subscribe to the idea that a positive belief system of empowering beliefs, aspirations and optimism are going to cure the afflictions of life. Nor does this book offer these as remedies to disease, trauma, tragedies, poverty or such associated elements of extreme deprivation.

What this book does offer, is to look at how the reader can observe, investigate, understand, confront and create choices to the mindset or mental frameworks with which he or she is dealing with the situation, circumstances or people representing them, including the self. This in order to seek, identify, examine, seize or leverage any opportunity as it presents itself to alter, change, redirect reframe or redesign the course of such journeys to deliver improved results and consequences. Using more open, curious, positively poised, goal focused and emotionally balanced mind frames in conjunction with a positively engaged spirit. Life is a series of experiments. This book asks the reader to believe in giving the self a strong positive disposition to engage with life in an increasingly collaborative way of the head, heart and hands.

An Indicative List of Values

Achievement Action bias Adaptability Adventure Ambition Assertiveness Authenticity Autonomy

Balance Beauty Boldness Broad-mindedness

Calmness Career Caring Challenge Clarity Comfort Compassion Competence Competition Confidence Conscientiousness Consideration Contentment Contribution Cooperation Courage Creativity Curiosity Customer Care

Dependability Determination Diligence Discipline

Honesty Intimacy Joy Kindness Knowledge Leadership Learning Love / affection Loyalty Methodical Meticulousness Modesty Nurturing Others Growth oriented

Open-mindedness Optimism/Optimistic Organized Originality Obedient

Patience Passionate Peace loving Perseverance Personal growth Politeness Power Pragmatic Precision Productive Professionalism Progressive Prosperity Minded Punctuality Purposefulness

Quality Conscious Quickness

Recognition Resourcefulness Respect Responsibility Risk taking

Security Self-control Sensibility Service Simplicity Sincerity Sociability Social responsibility Spirituality Status Strength Structure / clarity Success

Talent Teamwork Tolerance Trustworthiness Truthfulness

Understanding Uniqueness

Value Variety Versatility Victory Vigour

Warmth Willpower Wisdom Wit

NOTES ON EMOTIONAL INTELLIGENCE

EMOTIONAL INTELLIGENCE (EQ)

EQ is the ability to understand and use our emotions in a positive and constructive way. It's about engaging others in ways that brings out the best in them while building strong relationships.

Everyday EQ

"Everyday EQ" looks at creating effective

everyday competencies

To intersect and integrate our lives, hopes and dreams

with those we live and work with

When we can positively engage, energize and influence others in an everyday way, we can influence the future of our world everyday

- Dexter Valles

VALMAR INTERNATIONAL

EQ is also about understanding our own emotional state, the emotional states of others, and having clear influential communication.

Emotional Intelligence is often thought of as a description of your capability to manage your emotions effectively. However, Emotional Quotient or EQ is a measurement of how emotionally savvy you are. This is measured across emotional competencies which indicate what is being measured too. It is important that you work toward developing a wholesome development of emotional competence across all the EQ competencies.

EQ Competencies are most easily understood through the famed Six Seconds' EQ Competencies Model often called the KCG Model of EQ, Where it comprises 3 Key Pursuits: Know Yourself (Awareness of the range of Emotions you experience and Your Patterns of Behaviour) , Choose Yourself (Intentionality and the ability to pause, think about consequences and make better choices while remaining optimistic and motivated) and Give Yourself (Finding Purpose through Contributing with Empathy to the world, what you wish to receive from it. In short, building the world you want to live in)

Understanding the imbalances and shortcomings in your emotional competence make-up can give you great insight why you fall into emotional traps and why you make some decisions you are likely to regret later.

Your areas of strength in your bag of emotional competencies can help you develop your overall EQ savvy-ness by leveraging these strengths of your emotional character. As the Captain of your Ship of Life, others too depend on you to leverage these strengths on the rough seas of emotions.

How Our Beliefs Determine Life

The 2020 Assault on Life, need to be managed with exceptional emotional skill of those who lead the business and society. This is not the best place for the faint hearted to be in the most terrifying storm of the century. Courageous, Competent Leaders of Character forged in the fires of raging emotions need to lead the charge of humanity into the future.

You need to believe that you are that kind of leader. It's a Way of Life ! Unlock it with the strength and power of an emotionally powerful life.

Reading & Reference Resource :
World Leaders in Applied EQ and the largest EQ Network in the world
Six Seconds USA   www.6seconds.org

Note : Emotional Intelligence was first written about extensively by Dr Daniel Goleman in 1995. He is often referred to as the Founding Father of Emotional Intelligence. You can visit https://www.danielgoleman.info/

The Purpose of our Emotions	
Joy	Achieve goals, expand possibilities
Fear	Puts us on Alert about Uncertainty, Unknown
Anger	Obstacle, Need for change
Sadness	Unachieved goal, Loss of loved ones
Acceptance	Recognize Value, Openness
Anticipation	Planning Ahead, New situation
Disgust	Unacceptable, reject/move away
Surprise	Different from reality, re-evaluate

Source : Six Seconds USA. www.6seconds.org

How Our Beliefs Determine Life

A Useful Feelings List

Accepting / Open
Calm
Centered
Content
Fulfilled
Patient
Peaceful
Present
Relaxed
Serene
Trusting

Aliveness / Joy
Amazed
Awe
Bliss
Delighted
Eager
Ecstatic
Enchanted
Energized
Engaged
Enthusiastic
Excited
Free
Happy
Inspired
Invigorated
Lively
Passionate
Playful
Radiant
Refreshed
Rejuvenated
Renewed
Satisfied
Thrilled
Vibrant

Angry / Annoyed
Agitated
Aggravated
Bitter
Contempt
Cynical
Disdain
Disgruntled
Disturbed
Edgy
Exasperated
Frustrated
Furious
Grouchy
Hostile
Impatient
Irritated
Irate
Moody
On edge
Outraged
Pissed
Resentful
Upset
Vindictive

Courageous / Powerful
Adventurous
Brave
Capable
Confident
Daring
Determined
Free
Grounded
Proud
Strong
Worthy
Valiant

Connected / Loving
Accepting
Affectionate
Caring
Compassion
Empathy
Fulfilled
Present
Safe
Warm
Worthy
Curious
Engaged
Exploring
Fascinated
Interested
Intrigued
Involved
Stimulated

Despair / Sad
Anguish
Depressed
Despondent
Disappointed
Discouraged
Forlorn
Gloomy
Grief
Heartbroken
Hopeless
Lonely
Longing
Melancholy
Sorrow
Teary
Unhappy
Upset
Weary
Yearning

Disconnected / Numb
Aloof
Bored
Confused
Distant
Empty
Indifferent
Isolated
Lethargic
Listless
Removed
Resistant
Shut Down
Uneasy
Withdrawn

Embarrassed /
Shame
Ashamed
Humiliated
Inhibited
Mortified
Self-conscious
Useless
Weak
Worthless

Fear
Afraid
Anxious
Apprehensive
Frightened
Hesitant
Nervous
Panic
Paralyzed
Scared
Terrified
Worried

Fragile
Helpless
Sensitive

Grateful
Appreciative
Blessed
Delighted
Fortunate
Grace
Humbled
Lucky
Moved
Thankful
Touched

Guilt
Regret
Remorseful
Sorry

Hopeful
Encouraged
Expectant
Optimistic
Trusting

Powerless
Impotent
Incapable
Resigned
Trapped
Victim

Tender
Calm
Caring
Loving
Reflective
Self-loving
Serene
Vulnerable
Warm

Stressed / Tense
Anxious
Burned out
Cranky
Depleted
Edgy
Exhausted
Frazzled
Overwhelmed
Rattled
Rejecting
Restless
Shaken
Tight
Weary
Worn out

Unsettled / Doubt
Apprehensive
Concerned
Dissatisfied
Disturbed
Grouchy
Hesitant
Inhibited
Perplexed
Questioning
Rejecting
Reluctant
Shocked
Sceptical
Suspicious
Unsure
Worried

SOURCE : https://www.hoffmaninstitute.org/

ABOUT DEXTER

Professionally Certified Life & Executive Coach

(Results Coaching Systems & International Coach Federation @ 2008- Level 1 certified & Professional Coaching @ Coaching Lighthouse @ 2019)

Internationally Certified ENNEAGRAM Personality Profiling @ 2009(Certified by Jerome Wagner)

Internationally Certified Emotional Intelligence Practitioner, EQ Vital Signs Consultant, Certified EQ – Assessor & Coach @ 2010, 2011, 2012, 2013 (Certified by Six Seconds , California)

Internationally Certified MiND Practitioner @ 2016 (Certified by MyBrain International Limited, UK)

DEXTER J VALLES

A Profile

An International Business Professional, a Life & Executive Coach, *Acclaimed Corporate Master Trainer & a Professor of Management Studies* , across an extensive career founded over an absorbing 32 years with Global and Indian markets

Dexter is considered one of India's leading EQ consultants, specializing in the crucial area of *neuroscience based Emotional Intelligence EQ competencies* applied to Life & Leadership. He is a multi-certified EQ Practitioner, EQ Assessor and Organizational EQ Vital Signs consultant helping people and organizations connect life & work competencies to hidden behavioural drivers

Coaching has been a pursuit of passion for the past 10 years, ever since certifying as a Coach first in 2008. The desire was to enable people reach their goals way beyond the *"classroom of learning" into* the streets of life and the aspirations at their workplaces.

Empaneled as Lead Learning Facilitator, over 20 years Dexter has facilitated and coached dreams and desires, developing competence of several thousands of participants across the globe through innumerable training workshops with several key Indian and Multinational Corporate Houses

You can contact Dexter Valles here

DEXTER JOHN VALLES
CEO & Managing Consultant, Valmar International
Founder Director, The EQ Legion of India

Facebook https://www.facebook.com/dexvalles
LinkedIn
https://www.linkedin.com/in/dextervalles
Twitter @dynamodex
Website 1 http://www.valmarinternational.com
Website 2
https://dextervalles.wixsite.com/website
Email : dexter@valmarinternational.com

Recommended Reading, References and Credits

This book is wholly and completely an original work drawn from my own experiences and experiments in life. Along with a lot of reading up on life along the way.

These books and their authors in particular inspired me to put my thoughts and beliefs together and write this book. I highly recommend that you read these books.

The Secret by Rhonda Byrne
The Magic by Rhonda Byrne
E Squared by Pam Grout
E Cubed by Pam Grout
The Brain-The Story of You by Davis Eagleman

Additional Recommended Reading- some other books which have influenced me on this particular pathway:

Man's Search For Meaning by Viktor Frankl
Daring Greatly by Brene Brown
Emotional Intelligence and Working With Emotional Intelligence by Daniel Goleman (besides all his other books including The Brain and Emotional Intelligence)

Dexter's VIDEO Talks

We invite you to watch these interesting videos

Perceiving Reality
https://youtu.be/fG4kGk_IOiA
Perception and Reality are often debated to understand what's really true. Is there anything like Reality? Is it all Perception. Well it all depends on how they matter and to whom. Does Reality exist by itself? Is information and data useful if not processed in context to a framework? The same goes for Reality! Perceiving Reality on our own context sets up the world to be judged by us. Based on our assumptions and filters of our experiences. We have an image or perception or preconceived expectation of ourselves to begin with, others around us, how the world works and how it should. All this makes up for an interesting life executing our judgements and decisions on which we act.

Engaging the Energy of Life
https://youtu.be/4y35QrrO8qg
We drag ourselves around our lives with just about enough energy to reach the end of the day. How much are we paying Mindful attention to what our energy is creating or blocking? Developing energy that vibrates at higher frequencies creates positive attraction, attention, connection and influence. We create the energy field we operate within and connect with the world. And therefore we create the world we live in.

Connecting with Purpose Everyday
https://youtu.be/fU0I5YUo8hc
Everyday we are busy with the actions that make up life. Our goals and plans collide with the reality of each day. We strive, we cope, we do. Endlessly. But how much of it has meaning ? How

131

does it connect with our purpose. The reason we live. The person we are. Who we want to truly be. Can everyday contribute in a small way to our future ? Can we get to that happy place where we know everyday that we have done something that is worthwhile and meaningful? Can we communicate that to ourselves to energize our lives, in place of the exhaustion and exasperation with our" human doing" rather than "human being" !

Leading Success with your Heart
https://youtu.be/TPadHbXiBt8
What's your Mantra for Success ? How do you balance Power, Success, Performance and People ? Merging the Mind with the Heart allows one to lead with Competence and also with Compassion, Courage and Character. It helps deliver outstanding results and create powerful relationships. Aligning Vision and Purpose with managing People, Performance and Practices. Coherence of Head, Heart and Hands.

The Sigma of Presentation Skills
https://youtu.be/SI-EzwnHm6o
Make a great first impression ! But how?? !! Butterflies in the stomach, the mind blanking out, being transfixed or stuttering at the start could be your doom ! So use the SIGMA way to make a great start. One which will put you at ease and give you the confidence to make a great presentation. Of course there's a lot more to Presentation Design and Delivery. We shall keep that for another time !!

Communicating Assertively
https://youtu.be/fWlKh-3eOH8
Our relationships influence the nature and quality of our communication. Assertiveness as a way of life is about being clear, firm and fair in communicating our intentions first and our

behaviour based on securing an equitable result for everyone as much as possible. It's not possible to do this all the time, but if it is a large part of how we behave, people will ultimately respond in similar ways. Investing in relationships is a good way to call on them to address the needs of all people in the relationship. This does not mean that new or brief relationships need witness a free-for-all brawl or mute acceptance. It just means that when we practice assertiveness enough, it comes through in even the smaller moments of life. Our intentions get curated to a level at which even if communication breaks down, people feel safe enough to continue the conversation.

Live Life Beyond Learning & Assessments
https://youtu.be/jbi6CBl9K2E

Many among us would have received feedback on ourselves. As students our report cards served as feedback. As corporate citizens it's our performance assessment and conversations with our seniors. As adult learners we get various inputs from learning programs, learning models, audits and assessments - psychometric and others. Putting it all together can be quite a task. Perhaps we should just be listening in rather than being handcuffed to these. Filling in the blanks into our blindside can be useful. Does not mean we discard everything we know or think we know about ourselves. Rather we can use such inputs to also clarify, validate and curate the info we have. Remember that our lives are across a canvas far greater than the assessment windows and models which look at certain specific aspects of our lives in an interesting and insightful way. We are larger than the data. And the context within which we operate our lives is more dynamic. Let the context not suffer from the content. Yet let the content inform the context too!

How Our Beliefs Determine Life

Masks & Me
https://youtu.be/AogKMdbzAv8
Do you wear a mask? Yes we all do for different reasons. Most of them are to project an image. How authentic are we when for every good reason we project who we wish to be than who we really are? What is the benefit and how much does it cost us? How can we close the gap between the authentic self and the projected self? When can we evolve to authentically be the mask we wear?

Learn Life's Lessons Everyday
https://youtu.be/ptZP3zaMsCg
Everyday provides us moments of truth which indicate lessons we can use to make life better. Even the smallest lesson can turn to deliver the greatest benefit. How much are you paying attention to what your life and experiences are telling you?

Dance to Lifes' Music
https://youtu.be/HFZFB3HnO28
Everyday we live, we learn. Capture each lesson consciously. Share it with others. We live very different lives but surprisingly have very similar needs. The music of our lives can help other people dance through theirs !

Life is All Around You. Are you Present ?
https://youtu.be/LDuuuECIGd8
We hurry through life, trying to get to the other side. Success and Happiness. They are all somehow only in the Future. Can we notice the moment we are in ? What are we ignoring and perhaps losing in our race to the future ? When that too becomes the present, will we race through it too ? Arriving numbed and dazed at the end of life ?

The Steering Wheel of Life-Edited
https://youtu.be/W0KdbtKwX6Q

Do you feel in control of life only when you are driving it? Are your hands locked on the steering wheel. Are you driving blind through traffic. Is there a chance you could fall asleep at the wheel? How do we deal with handing over the wheel to someone else? Is it always our car and our destination that matters? What do we need to consider on the shared journey of life such that we live as fully as possible in the moment whilst creating the future?

Steering Wheel & You !
https://youtu.be/yr4UTMy_UJ4

At the Steering Wheel of Life are you driving people Nuts??!! Is your focus so single minded that you drive by the moment and the magic of the process to a destination that denies you the journey itself? What does it mean to be obsessed with controlling the wheel of your life and all those in your car? At work how connected are you with your team? Are they empowered to drive your car? At home, are you so fixated at the wheel that it doesn't matter where others want to go, as long as they are going with you? How much will it take to unlock your grip from the wheel and embrace the journey together with others?

Driving Performance Excellence-Edited
https://youtu.be/FKHxgvzxWt8

Four Key Performance Drivers explained.

Our success lies in how we perform. How we perform lies in what drives us. What drives us depends on what motivates us and others. Motivation depends a lot on our emotional energy and our relationships with people we wish to impact with our performance

How Our Beliefs Determine Life

! We take a look at 4 Key Drivers : Communicating with Impact & Influence, Managing a Changing Environment, Performing through People with Empathy and Making a Personal Difference.

The Art of Winning Arguments
https://youtu.be/Z5xqVtBUNZc

Most of the time in the rush to decide things, our conversations, discussions and debates turn into Win-Lose Arguments. There are victors and there are the vanquished. Relationships fall apart. So perhaps we need to revisit the words we are using to describe these conversations in our minds. The way we position ourselves. The stances we adopt. The emotions were engage with. And the traffic jams of our collective egos we are stuck in.

Winning "Arguments" without Losing Relationships. Needs you to Change your Language, Reframe Communication, Take Responsibility, Enlist support, Engage Empathy and convert arguments into productive high energy courageous conversations.

Asserting your EQ
https://youtu.be/LHwsTi9p0Q0

Assertiveness is the key to EQ. Communicating is crucial to managing Relationships and Results. Communicating with Emotional Balance is how we demonstrate emotional intelligence. Powerful, trustworthy, authentic and reliable relationships help us get to the results we desire. Assertiveness is a critical milestone on pathway to an EQ life!

The Code of the Road
https://youtu.be/pPvjbB_A7zk

The roads we travel on and the traffic we negotiate everyday

are uncannily like life itself. Here we take a look at what quick lessons we can learn on the roads of life and put them to work in life itself.
Music credit : Dreamy Dreamers by Samsung Galaxy A50s mobile phone video editing software

Claim your Rightful Life
https://youtu.be/1TlBeKJIoml

Little things do matter. The permissions you give define the quality of your life. Announce your Life is about claiming your right to a life that is fair, just, equitable and civil. It's about setting your boundaries. We teach others how to treat us by the way we treat ourselves. We need to stand up, smile and say something! Because it matters !!

Who are you ?
https://youtu.be/i1MdAIr9AIc

We often define our lives by what we do. Yet we are not truly products of our profession or qualifications or achievements. That's why some people great success stories are riddled with doubt and unhappy with their lives. Finding out the answer to Who You Are can help find Purpose and redefine your life. Or of course endorse your life. Either way, it's good to answer the question Who Are You !

Engaging EQ Energy
https://youtu.be/b9M-VapoAN4

This is the first Episode in the series Engaging EQ Energy. It's about understanding Emotional Intelligence, the role of emotions themselves, the EQ Framework and How one can engage the 3 Pursuits of the EQ Competences as defined by Six Seconds, California, USA, world leaders in the study and application of EQ.

LESSONS FROM THE CROSS OF CRISIS
https://youtu.be/wXLvfAi5mxl

Every crisis has several lessons to learn from. Currently the world is plunged into the chaos of the Coronavirus Crisis. Our very existence is threatened. Panic has taken over the reins of what we once knew to be a regulated, planned and organized life. Pressing the Pause Button has put the world face to face with the most dreadful reality of our times. Yet there are compelling lessons to learn as we survive this gut wrenching turbulence. Five Lessons emerge with practical wisdom which we can harness to negotiate our passage through life.

Making Relationships Count
https://youtu.be/qIKMHckXWW0

We are often held hostage by our friendships and relationships. Burdened by the responsibility of managing the imbalances and inequities of the relationship. Taking the blame in order to keep the peace. An unfair friendship is destructive. Manipulative relationships make doormats of people who are unwilling to call out the unfairness and have conversations about how it needs to be. Beware of being a victim or victimizing others in friendships where too much is being asked of the other almost all of the time.

Fingerprinting Success
https://youtu.be/QCucf5n-1G0

Just as our fingerprint is an unique identification of each of us as individuals, success too has an unique DNA or Fingerprint of how we engage our Values, our Goals and our Emotions which hold them together and give them life and direction.

It's all in our hands, literally and figuratively!! Here we look at an interesting way to count our Values and Goals on our fingers and look at what we hold in the palms of our hands. Our Core Values and Our Vision which together script the Legacy of our Lives

REWIRING Life Beyond COVID-19
https://youtu.be/co_uA-fZoGA

The world is under siege and we are besieged with the fear of the unknown and unseen. Never before have we had to change the context of our lives so dramatically.

We can take this time and opportunity to rewire and reimagine our lives beyond the uncertainty and disruption we are struggling to live through.

To REFRAME our lives is to recreate the context within which we operate, moving from Panic & Paralysis to Productivity.

R : Review & Reflect on what are thoughts are in the moment
E : Engagement Levels of our Emotions and Actions
F : Focus on FIVE important issues
R : Draw up a Rewiring Plan.
A : Activate the Plan
M : Measure Progress, Mend the Plan to work better
E : Educate, Enlarge & Energize your Reframed life

Locked Down & Locked Into Life
https://youtu.be/GIqaSCqqw4w

Learning to deal with the lockdown allows us to revisit our lives.

How Our Beliefs Determine Life

And learn as students of the game, once again. Stay Home Stay Safe and Stay a Student of Life. This is Life sending us Back to School !

Living a Re-Loaded Life !
https://youtu.be/0VuMZWsGIps

The old ways die away as we learn to cope in the new world of 2020. This is a year we shall never forget. Stories shall be told of how we fought the Coronavirus and survived How the world stopped its mad dash to an insane future. How we recreated or were forced to recreate the world which we had dismantled and almost destroyed. Let's make sure we are part of that story. Let's give ourselves reasons to succeed Time to think how we need to revitalize old ways, values and behaviour to succeed in the new context that this scourge has thrown to recast the very vitality of life

Lockdown into your Legacy_ Rewrite your Story
https://youtu.be/7NZ_KXPEPPk

Use the coronavirus lockdown to look into rewriting the story of your life. Thread the significant moments of your life and see how your story had developed and defined life. Most of us have lived significant lives in many ways. Let's take that forward and leave a legacy. Something that lives beyond us as a gift to those who follow. This year 2020 is a landmark year in human history. Let it scare us to survive and thrive with renewed vigour and vitality. Let new powerful stories emerge beyond the lockdown ! Unlock the amazing stories from rest of your life !

The Power of Your Life Story !
https://youtu.be/n-54JHAgrF0

Our life is on Pause. It is the perfect gift of time and opportunity to look into rewriting the story of your life. Stitch the significant moments of your life driven by powerful emotions and see how your story had developed and defined life. What is the DNA of your life ? How is it going to help you ? This year 2020 is a landmark year in human history. Let new powerful stories emerge beyond the lockdown ! Emerge from the shadows to the light of the life of the future you are scripting today.

OTHER BOOKS BY THIS AUTHOR

INSPIRED BY
THE HOLY SPIRIT

Available on www.amazon.com in Kindle and Paperback

The
Butterfly
Blueprint

Managing
Transformative Change

Dexter Valles

THE BUTTERFLY BLUEPRINT
Managing Transformative Change

Metamorphosis is an incredibly fascinating journey of transitioning the ordinary caterpillar to a magnificent butterfly! It needs patience and care. Just as our own life must go through metamorphosis from helplessness to strength, from being unskilled and inept to being skilled and agile! Yet in our impatience we often wake up the Caterpillar in ourselves and others too, halfway through the metamorphosis, hoping that the butterfly within has already formed

Even before any of the magic has been displayed, we want this butterfly to grow its wings and fly. Our competitive speeding world in which we live today, brings us breathlessly close to the threshold of destroying the cocoon and the magical metamorphosis within it.
Every caterpillar must bide its' time to be born a butterfly. The butterfly too, must be released from the memories of the cocoon, to fly gracefully in fields of flowers. The lessons from the cocoon are now invisible part of butterfly beauty and grace. That's the Butterfly Blueprint ! The Cocoon meets the Sky !

We take a look at what it means to design, engage and coach the Butterfly Blueprint. This book deals with this journey in Four Parts. Beginning with the Caterpillar, it's Metamorphosis, and finally the Butterfly ! To converge the Blueprint to everyday actions and advice, we Engage the Blueprint into FIVE Focus Areas in the Butterfly Blueprint's Flight

@

THE STEERING WHEEL OF LIFE
Success Scripts

This book has several Success Scripts on various aspects of life Each article has its very own precious nugget of wisdom. Beginning with ASPIRE for Success, the book leads you through a gallery of rich portraits of life like Leading on the Edge, Eekonomics -Managing in Tough Times, Leading & Engaging Emotional Energy – Emotional Intelligence practical wisdom and practices, an interestingly christened article The Street Clothes of Respect, Relating with Emotional Purpose which looks at crafting Successful Relationships and several more gems to add sparkle and paint to the portrait of a successful life.

These Success Scripts have been compiled to offer the reader an opportunity to design a Personal Success Script after learning from the insights in each article.

No Success Script is final and absolute. Each one must write and rewrite their scripts to meet the changing times and life experiences while steering the ship of their lives across the seas and oceans of change.

It is a compilation of such wisdom-pods which can appeal and relate to different people for different reasons. And to you too, at different points of your life.

You must ultimately write your own success script. That's when you shall take charge of the wheel and steer the ship of your life to the wide-open seas of success.

THE CODE OF THE ROAD
Navigating Life's Traffic Lanes

This book is a product of my everyday life, driving around in the heavily congested roads of my beloved city Mumbai in INDIA

I would end my day feeling an overwhelming rush of mixed emotions and found it really hard to shrug off the strong connections to everyday Life ! As I reflected on what I could learn from these experiences, interesting relationships began to form and make strange sense to me.

All travelers have encountered Roadblocks along their journeys. The 5 Road Block Lessons offer interesting insight into the usefulness of Roadblocks on the Road of Life. Navigating Life's Traffic Lanes takes you through 12 Lane Laws of Life each translated into a cryptic Life Lesson.

The Road of Life as you shall discover, is governed by The Code of the Road. The book takes you on a road trip through three segments – Your Car, The Road and The Code putting it all together in a delightful summary called You, The Road and the Code. Enjoy the Ride !

CONNECTED TO SOUL
Igniting Human Spirit with Purpose

This book explores the essence of life and the human spirit connected to the soul. That eternal part of us which ignites our purpose and passion. This creates meaning drawn from what we do and allows us leave a Legacy. This Legacy rides forward on that fuel of Purpose with Passion long after we have stopped stoking the fire ourselves.

 Man is eternally in search of two major engines to drive life. The Engines of Purpose and Provision. These create direction and meaning. The truth is that one does not often find both together. Yet either one has the power to deeply engage the human spirit.

Engaging Energy or Passion would depend on where the engagement lies. Together these engines enable us engage the incredible and enormous power of an ignited life!

The journey of this book winds across 3 Parts. Each Part has 4 Ways of looking at the theme of that part. The chapters in each part describe their story of this book in their own unique ways. As if each chapter is written from a different view of life. In a way, as a reader you get 12 different views of the book, almost just like life is most of the time. Together they bring to the reader, the essence of the entire story of the book itself.

FLAWED yet PRECIOUS
Leading a Sparkling Life

As time flows by, we often look back at all the years gone by, and strive to understand what life has taught us. What can we do better? What would really need to be New in the coming Year?? What needs to change?

I feel it's more about incremental steps of self-revelation. Peeling off the onion rings. Increasing vulnerability. In the place of numbness. I realize that as long as we find our way to live with integrity, strip the deceit and strive for authenticity in our lives , be mindful of our behaviour as we relate with others, and develop deeper consciousness of who we are in each moment; we can evolve to be the person in every essence we truly are and meant to be.

We can then relate to others in ways that release them to be and live the luminous lives they too are.

While this may seem complex in the way we practice living, tiptoeing around our realities, adding layers of interpretations to what's in plain sight, in truth, the simpler we make our everyday explanations the easier they are to access and engage across the experiences we create for ourselves and others. And here's the shocker. We can guarantee mistakes!! But you see, that's how we are too... Flawed yet precious. Flawed in our human-ness, Precious in the divinity of our dreams and aspirations nurtured within

LEADERSHIP IMPERATIVES
Living & Leading Beyond 2020

The landscape of the world has changed dramatically since Covid-19 hit our lives. This is perhaps the most Metamorphic Transformation of the world we have ever witnessed in our lifetime. Stories shall be told about these days throughout history. We are part of those stories. They are about how we stood up and were counted. How lives and livelihood were protected and promoted. How business design and strategy evolved to reshape and reframe the future. And how Leadership emerged from the darkness of the Lockdown to shine brightly in the sky.

Like the Sun. Burning away inequalities and inequities of the past, and growing a planet of people determined to survive, thrive and flourish, together! This book is about how that can happen. These are the pages which describe the making of this New Earth History!

This History of our Future, as chronicled in these pages is written with a Vision of the unfolding of time. As it is read, it comes to life, and builds the case for a reimagined look at Leadership beyond the Lockdown across 3 Parts of a living chronicle : Landscapes of Change, New Scripts driving Success which embrace "Now and Disruptive Change" being life partners and Leadership Imperatives which focus on Four Glorious Leaders or Leadership Personas

In particular, The Warrior Leader is an absorbing tale of Strong Goal Oriented Leadership, using the aspects of PURCHASE to put it together. Rainbow Reasoning is a remarkable rewriting of strategic decision making, really new to thinking beyond the established Black, White & Grey ways of the past. History is being rewritten with the full spectrum of Colour.

No doubt Digital Leadership will take center stage and as predicted in this book shall dominate most business conversations and strategies for the entire foreseeable future. Yet EQ Savvy Leadership and Spirit Centered Leadership must keep the heart and soul of leadership invested in people, in what can become a runaway artificially intelligent insular, clinically efficient and de-humanized world.

Reading this book not only informs us about the future of times to come, but creates the future with the turn of each page ! Enjoy your part in living and rewriting the History of the World !

THE WARRIOR LEADER
Inspire. Influence. Ignite

This book looks at life through the eyes of leadership. A leadership with a special style. Not just to lead with, but to live with. This is the Warrior Leader. Fierce. Focused. Courageous. Competent. Compassionate. And importantly, Visionary. Versatile. Resilient. Ignited. Agile.

A Lethal array of Arrows in the Warrior Leader's Quiver. To pierce through the darkness and storm of turbulence, chaos and disruption. To reach the distant verdant hills of a flourishing life-scape which hold the heart of hope that yearns to beat once again in the bosom of humanity.

The Warrior Leader is an absorbing tale of Strong Goal Oriented Leadership, leveraging Four Attributes : Visionary, Versatile, Resilient, and Lethal

These Four Attributes are innate to a Warrior Leader. Almost like the DNA Genetic Code of such leaders. They often operate unconsciously from these when faced with crisis or crisis like circumstances. You can sense the energy radiate around a Warrior Leader and will find yourself bathed in that aura. Nothing seems too difficult or desperate when a Warrior Leader leads the way. Almost magically the world becomes better, safer and happier.

It's now time to realize that that very magic lies within each one of us. The Warrior Leader lives in each one of us. This book helps you create your very own Agile Warrior Leader's Battlefield Blueprint. You must put this book down only when you have done that. Make that promise to your future !

5 FLAGS OF LIFE

Dexter Valles

5
FLAGS
OF LIFE

The Essence of Living
and Leading Today

Dexter Valles

5 FLAGS OF LIFE
The Essence of Living and Leading Today

The Flag is probably the oldest symbol of identity, representation, honour, pride, presence and conquest. It has been used for various reasons ever since the time it was first raised as a military symbol and as a representation of national identity.

The Flag has been used to communicate both the tangible and intangible in everyday conversation. You would have used it often enough yourself. To Unfurl the Flag as a symbol of pride, hope and unique identity, to Plant the Flag in conquest, to Fly the Flag in defiance , bravado, mastery or even to surrender, to Raise the Flag on issues, to Flag Off a race, to Salute the Flag with Respect, to Keep the Flag Flying in continuous mastery and dominance.

The 5 Flags of Life are each of these and all of these. Each Flag is a symbol of your growing identity, prowess, pride, hope, dominance, mastery, conquest, respect.

Plant, Raise, Unfurl, Fly and Salute each Flag to create your unique identity and presence in life.

And finally, design your very own flag ! One which emblazons your identity with pride, for the world to recognize and acknowledge.

Made in the USA
Columbia, SC
23 October 2022

69882056R00087